# Communities Panchayats and Governance at Grassroots

## About the Authors

Prof. **Ganapathi Palanithurai**, Coordinator in Rajiv Gandhi Chair, Gandhigram Rural Institute, presently heads the Department of Political Science and Development Administration, Gandhigram Rural University, Tamil Nadu. He is also Associated with Centre Planning Commission, State Planning Commission of Tamil Nadu, Population Foundation of India, Ford Foundation, UNICEF, Rajiv Gandhi Foundation, CAPART, Ministry of Rural Areas and Employment and DANIDA (Danish-Indo Development Agency) in specific areas of activities in connection with empowerment of people.

Prof. Palanithurai has to his credit twenty-nine books and seventy-five articles on three major areas, namely, legislative behaviour, ethnicity and Panchayati Raj system. He was recipient of Fellowship from Sastri Indo-Canadian Institute, New Delhi and World Academy of Art and Science, USA. He is the Chairman of the Tamil Nadu Council for Sustainable Livelihoods. He was a visiting fellow in the MiGill University, Canada in 1989. He is a member of the expert committee constituted by the Government of Tamil Nadu to monitor the training programme for local body leaders.

Dr. V. **Ragupathy**, Reader in Political Science and Development Administration and Associate Coordinator, Rajiv Gandhi Chair for Panchayati Raj Studies Gandhigram Rural University Gandhigram Tamil Nadu, is an active academician working in the area of Panchayati Raj along with Prof. G. Palanithurai. Since he hails from a Gandhian family background his perspective towards the poor is visible.

He has done extensive research in the field of Panchayati Raj and Management of common property resources and he has contributed a number of research article published in reputed journals. He has actively participated as resource person in all training exercises done in Rajiv Gandhi Chair for Panchayat leaders and officials. He is involved in many action research projects funded by National and International Agencies. He is associated with many Gandhian Institutions in Tamil Nadu. He is an honorary Secretary of Gandhiniketan Ashram of T.Kallupatti, Madurai, Tamil Nadu.

# Communities Panchayats and Governance at Grassroots

G.Palanithurai
V. Ragupathy

CONCEPT PUBLISHING COMPANY, NEW DELHI-110059

**Cataloging in Publication Data—DK**
*Courtesy:* D.K. Agencies (P) Ltd. <docinfo@dkagencies.com>

Palanithurai, G. (Ganapathy), 1953-
Communities panchayats and governance at grassroots / G. Palanithurai, V. Ragupathy.
p. cm.
Study conducted in Tamil Nadu, India.
Includes bibliographical references.
Includes index.
ISBN 13: 9788180695636
ISBN 10: 8180695638

1. Panchayat—India—Tamil Nadu. 2. Direct democracy—India—Tamil Nadu 3. Water-supply—India—Tamil Nadu—Management—Citizen parti-cipation. 4. Natural resources—Co-management—India—Tamil Nadu. 5. Rural development—India—Tamil Nadu. I. Ragupathy, V. (Varadarajan), 1958- II. Title.

DDC 320.84 ) 954 82 22



ISBN-13: 978-81-8069-563-6
ISBN-10: 81-8069-563-8

First Published 2008



*Published and Printed by*
Ashok Kumar Mittal
**Concept Publishing Company**
A/15-16, Commercial Block, Mohan Garden
New Delhi-110059 (India)

*Phones* : 25351460, 25351794
*Fax* : 091-11-25357103
*Email* : publishing@conceptpub.com

To

The Divine Mother

# Preface

India had a rich tradition of self-governing institutions at the grassroots. The self-governing institutions were built up by a set of norms evolved by the communities. These laws were more social in character. Societal laws were more powerful than the laws of the State. An eminent historian, Radha Krishna Muherji, says, "In ancient India king was the head of the State but not of the society. He had a place in social hierarchy, but it was not of the highest place. As the symbol of the State be appeared to the people like a remote abstraction with no direct touch with their daily life, which was governed by the social organization".

At the dawn of independence Panchayati Raj became a subject of discussion and discourse as views expressed by M. K. Gandhi and Dr. B. R. Ambedkar were not the same but contradictory to each other. But both were realistic in their own perspective. Gandhi visualized a process to achieve a just society and Ambedkar projected the existing reality on the ground and hence local governance became a subject in the hands of the State Government under Article 40 of the Constitution of India. Over a period of time Panchayati Raj gained much attention as the centralized agencies lost their credibility and legitimacy in solving the basic issues of the poor, women and marginalized a period of forty years in independent India. In the process of governance and development people from the deprived and marginalized sections and women could not penetrate and as a result development brokers emerged from the political parties and they, in collaboration with bureaucracy dominate the society by getting things done for the poor. Ultimately poor have been reduced to dole receivers, beneficiaries and petitioners. To reverse the trend Rajiv Gandhi thought of an alternative paradigm by empowering the citizens through the new Panchayati Raj System.

Self-governance at the grassroots has been facilitated by the

73rd Constitutional Amendment Act. It also wants to restructure the existing discriminatory rural social structure and to include the traditionally excluded sections in the process of governance and development. There are opportunities, challenges and hurdles in operationalising the Panchayati Raj System. This tiny volume is an attempt to present the institutional pluralism at the grassroots and discuss how it affects the functioning of Panchayati Raj System.

The articles incorporated in this small monograph are field based studies. The villages selected for intensive study were visited by the research team several times. Intensive discussions were held with Gram Panchayat Presidents, community leaders, leaders of the marginalized, leaders of self-help groups and enough data were generated. Further data were collected from the records of the village Panchayats. Panchayat meetings, Gram Sabha meetings, community meetings and Community Sabha Meetings were attended by the research team of the Rajiv Gandhi Chair.

All the field activities were carried out by the research staff of the Rajiv Gandhi Chair for Panchayati Raj Studies. Since the Rajiv Gandhi Chair has been supported by the Ford Foundation, the UNDP, the World Bank, the State Planning Commission, the Ministry of Panchayati Raj, DANIDA and other agencies for its field-based activities and action research, we have twenty project staff in different projects involved in all the above activities. They have a grip over the field. Our theoretical discussion with the field staff enabled them to collect the needed data precisely. For all these articles the villages were visited several times and leaders were interviewed many times. Since our staff have got commitment, they have completed the task without any difficulty. We register our sincere thanks to them. Equally Gram Panchayat leaders, community leaders spared their valuable time with our research team for which we register our thanks to them also. Our colleagues and family members deserve our appreciation for having helped us in many ways to complete this work. We sincerely thank every one who has contributed to our academic pursuits.

Gandhigram
September 2007

**G. Palanithurai**
**V. Ragupathy**

# Contents

# List of Tables



# List of Diagrams

# 1
# Introduction

India is witnessing an unprecedented exercise of demo-cratizing the society and development through devolution of powers in the past one and half decade after the initiative taken by Rajiv Gandhi, the then Prime Minister of India, by enacting an Amendment to the Constitution of India. But this exercise is not smooth as the society is feudal, hierarchical, patriarchal and casteist. The struggle is on to break the hurdles and barriers created by those who enjoyed power and related benefits so far. Since the beneficiaries of the Amendments to the Constitution to devolve powers have formed a critical mass, the obstacles and barriers in the process are dismantled. For the first time in India democracy has reached the grassroots as a culture after the enactment of the 73rd and 74th Amendments to the Constitution of India. In India democracy is equated with elections and beyond that there was no serious step. No doubt, unlike other countries, especially the Western countries, India is known for its communitarian practices. Hence, however democratic it is, the practices of the communities are still in vogue and predominant. People were internalized on the provetices of the communities. Even after the enactment of the Constitution, many of the practices which were against the provisions of the Constitution, were in vogue. To remove all social evils there should be synergy between the practices of the community and social movements to reform society. In India activities have been very intense for political democracy and not for social democracy.

India is known for its paradoxes contradictions and diversities. No country in the world can be compared with India. In such a way India is unique and distinct. Many established theories have been proved to be wrong in India as Indian society and politics move in a unique direction and course. It is a wonderful social laboratory to evolve new theories and test old theories. The theory of democracy argues that, for the smooth running of democratic governance, social harmony is an imperative. Extreme social conflict will destablise democracy. But, in India, it is proved beyond doubt that, despite high social conflict, democracy survives successfully. India has achieved 9.5 per cent growth but it has gone down in human development from the 126th to the 128th place. Many established theories have been proved wrong in the Indian context.

It is believed that many of the social evils will be ended through the practice of the Constitution. But, in practice, many of the provisions of the Constitution have not reached the society as social laws are much more powerful than the constitutional laws among the people in the communities. With regard to social practices the Indian state is quiet soft. India is known for its progressive policies, decisions and laws. But in operationalising the same it is not so strong. Externally India is viewed positively from the perspective of adherence to international demands though enacting laws. Internally it is viewed negatively from the perspective of operationalising the laws decisions and politics. At present the Indian governing system has gone down in credibility as per the rating of governance by the citizens of the country. When constitutional provisions have gone down to the society, communities which have been oriented to democratic practices have accepted the changes due to the historic constitutional amendments. Communities which are still in the practice of community laws, refuse to adhere to the changes which are due to the Amendments. Of the three million representatives elected, one million are women and nearly twenty four per cent of them are from the Dalit communities. A new class of leaders has emerged from the last rung of the society. So far they were socially and economically deprived and were marginalized groups. In this context one has to concede the argument that communities are having some of the best practices which will enable the society to manage its affairs on its own. It is common to all societies. It is called social capital. One cannot outright reject the community practices.

Arguments were once projected that participatory democracy was the finest instrument of governance humanity ever evolved. Later it was argued that participatory democracy would yield results only in small units of governance. Territorially large societies require yet another vibrant form. Then representative democracy was hailed as one of the best forms of governance. At present again, the search is on for newer forms of governance. Participatory democracy through decentralized governance is being hailed as the best form in the context of globalization. Globalization and decentralization are viewed from opposite perspectives. In reality they are not working against each other. Any major event in the world will bring both positive and negative effects. Human societies, by their understanding, can take the best out of them. In the same way humanity, by its prudent action, has to take the positive and avoid the negative effects.

Thus globalization has brought in opportunities and threats. In the same way decentralization has both merits and demerits. One cannot find solutions to all the problems in decentralization and, in the same way, solutions cannot be found for all the issues in centralization. Both centralization and decentralization will work in harmony at appropriate levels. As stated above, constitutional laws and community laws are in practice. All Constitutional laws cannot produce the expected results in the community. Likewise all community laws are not producing positive results. We have an International Water Commission and a National Water Commission and yet water disputes have not been solved. But communities have water laws for sharing water. These formulas are ensuring perfect equity. This framework works effectively and settles many problems. Effective natural resource management has been done only through community laws. Hence it is imperative to study the

Constitutional practices and community practices at the grassroots and observe where one finds a conflict between constitutional laws and social laws and where one finds synergy between constitutional laws and social laws.

The Rajiv Gandhi Chair for Panchayati Raj Studies is continuously working for strengthening grassroots democracy and, while doing so, it has its own perspective to strengthen the social capital. While protecting the social capital, equity and equality and social justice were the key non-negotiable elements. Against this background studies conducted on these areas are brought together as a compendium for readers. There are seven articles prepared by the authors for presentation on different platforms. After the presentation, based on the community and observations, all the articles were revised.

G. Palanithurai's article "Constitutional Laws *Vs* Community Laws" brings to light the interaction between the two. Many times, on the ground, community laws establish their supremacy. It is a well-known fact that in the Afro-Asian countries community structures are so strong and they are able to deliver goods more effectively than the government. The traditional structures are in many countries positive towards delivering services. But they have their own drawbacks. To overcome the drawbacks in the traditional structure, constitutional structures are created. Yet they meet stiff resistance. The problems of the community laws and the advantages of the same are analyzed against the backdrop of the experience in other parts of the world. Traditional structures' merits and weaknesses are analyzed and reforms to be done in the traditional structures are also analyzed and indicated. In this article Palanithurai forcefully argues for a synergy between constitutional structures and traditional structures. The author's decisive observation is that the positive elements of the traditional structures have to be integrated with the constitutional panchayats.

G.Palanithurai's second article entitled "Synergisation of Traditional Panchayat with Formal Panchayati Raj System in

Managing the Community Affairs" is a field based study conducted in a Gram Panchayat which is a social laboratory for the Department of Political Science and Development Administration's outreach programmes. There are many Panchayats known for conflict between the traditional Panchayats and the constitutional Pancha-yats. Sometimes, in the struggle, constitutional Panchayats will emerge victorious by establishing their sway over the community. In certain places the community Panchayats establishes their supremacy over the constitutional Panchayats. Whatever happens on the ground it is with the support of the people. Rarely we find synergy between the traditional Panchayats and constitutional Panchayats. Karisalpatti is a Gram Panchayat in Dindigul District which has got several awards for outstanding service rendered to the community. In this gram panchayat the traditional Panchayat and the constitutional Panchayat have joined together and share responsibilities in discharging duties. Factors which are responsible for bringing synergy and conflict are analysed in this article.

Yet another article "Panchayats in Ground Water Management" written by G. Palanithurai speaks volumes about the role of Gram Panchayats in ground water management based on a field survey. He explains in detail the powers and responsibilities entrusted to the Gram Panchayats as per the Tamil Nadu Panchayat Act, 1994 and reports a field study in eleven Gram Panchayats. The article brings to light the initiatives of the Gram Panchayat Presidents in managing water resources. It is unequivocally demonstrated in Tamil Nadu that the Presidents who have done excellent work in water management have merged successfully and got recognition among the community. For effective ground water management, the support of the communities is essential. The author highlights the efforts of the Gram Panchayats in evolving a framework to prepare a natural resources management plan.

V. Ragupathy's article "Common Property Resource Management in Panchayati Raj—Status and Opportunities" tries to explain the reasons for the Tragedy of Commons in the world. With the help of the available theories on common property resource management, Ragupathy brings to light the conditions of the commons in India and particularly in Tamil Nadu. He points out that collectivities are affected due to poor management of the commons. Further he goes deep into the provisions of the Panchayati Raj Act to cover the management of the commons and analyses the problems involved in it. He indicates the conditions which are necessary for the effective management of the commons and against the above backdrop, he critically evaluates the provisions of the Panchayati Raj Act in Tamil Nadu. He suggests ways and means to strengthen the new Panchayati Raj System by plugging the loopholes in the existing Panchayati Raj Act in Tamil Nadu. His analysis is based on the theories of the commons.

The article "Social Liberation and Empowerment in Panchayats—Stages and Struggles in Tamil Nadu" by V.Ragupathy path-breakingly traces the process by which the marginalized moved into the corridors of power. He underlines the existing social conditions in which the Dalits and women are contesting in elections and shouldering responsibilities. To discharge the responsibilities and perform the roles the women and Dalit leaders have to face a volley of problems in the present context. He has drawn cases from Tamil Nadu and analyzed their problems contextually. Based on the existing literature, he has formulated the stages of empowerment. He indicates five states, namely rejection, tokenism, compromise, struggle and empowerment. He analyses the cases and indicates where and in what stage the leaders are in the process of empowerment. From the cases he fixes the key determinants of empowerment of Dalits. A new line of argument has been projected in this article which needs further validation and examination. The article provides scope for building a framework for meaningful analysis of empowerment of women and Dalits through the Panchayati Raj System.

G. Palanithurai's article entitled "Local Communities and

Water Management Issues" brings to light the conflict between the market and the communities over trading of water under globalization. Globalization has made the community's entitlement, 'water', a marketable and tradable commodity. Globalization has started working and shapes every activity towards the market and it ultimately affects the poor, the women and the marginalized. Water is the best case to demonstrate how these groups are affected due to globalization. Decentralisation has provided opportunity to the community to act appropriately to safeguard their endowments and thereby the communities can decide through the Panchayati Raj System whether market forces can be allowed to trade in water. By drawing cases from Tamil Nadu, the author has demonstrated how communities are able to resist the inroads of the multinational companies into the villages for water trade and how communities are opted into the process of water trade through the new Panchayati Raj System. Through this article the ill effects of globalization and decentralisation have been demonstrated. It needs further investigation and validation.

V. Ragupathy's article "Self-Governing Water Republics at the Granroot" is yet another write-up focused on the vibrancy of the communities in managing water. Sivaganga district is known for its economic backwardness and atrocities against the Dalits and equally known for the effective management of water by the community Panchayats. Sivaganga district is known for water scarcity also. The community Panchayats have their own regulations to manage water and they have a management framework to deal with water. He extensively refers to the studies conducted earlier on the same theme to fix the conditions under which the communities are made to have such a kind of institutional framework. He extensively cities the working of the community Panchayats in establishing their hold over the natural resources, especially water. In nearly 65 per cent of the villages water comes under the purview of the community Panchayats. Ragupathy also touches upon the interface between the community Panchayats and constitutional Panchayats. Even for this, he has drawn cases from Panchayats. This article leaves a lot of scope for further investigation and validation.

Through the above articles, the powers of the local communities have been demonstrated. The interface between the community Panchayats and constitutional Panchayats in managing the entitlements of the community has been demonstrated. Extensive analysis has been made based on the cases drawn from the field. Where both institutions meet and make for synergy and where they work apart are brought to light in all these articles. All these articles have brought several propositions for further probe and validation. The authors of the articles have moved into the established notions and brought out the realities. Normally scholars blindly go into these issues against the backdrop of the new Panchayati Raj System after the 73rd Amendment to the Constitution of India. But in this volume they have brought to light the existing realities from the perspectives of community Panchayats and constitutional Panchayats.

These articles leave a lot of scope for scholars from the anthropological and sociological perspective. There are many sociological and anthropological issues involved in the functioning of the Panchayati Raj System. Scholars are providing the issues of the Panchayati Raj System from a legalistic managerial and political perspective.

# 2

# Constitutional Laws *Vs* Community Laws

*G. Palanithurai*

## Introduction

The 73rd and the 74th Amendments to the Constitution of India have enabled the marginalized and the oppressed to move into the power structure in grassroots governance. The two amendments have a rich potential to transform and alter the nature of governance and social dynamics.[1] To realise the potential, the State has to play an effective role. Dalits got elected to local bodies but they are not allowed to function independently as leaders and discharge their responsibilities. Women got elected to local bodies and they are not allowed to sit in the office and discharge their responsibilities. In such a way barriers and obstacles are created by the leaders of traditional institutions.[2] They are drawn towards governance because seats have been reserved for Dalits and women. The constitution grants such opportunities but the community rejects them. Why this syndrome is a major question to be probed. The whole exercise is around the interface between the state created institutions and the community evolved institutions.

## Context

After the departure of the colonial power, the modern state system provided an institutional mechanism to govern and administer the society and achieve development based on the western model of Parliamentary democracy. The Afro-Asian countries borrowed this model and adopted the same without much adaptation to suit the local conditions. The Afro-African countries are known for their strong traditional structures for community governance. One would find strong resistance to reform in certain aspects of the society and more particularly on governance. That is why we find a new syndrome of modernity in tradition and tradition in modernity in many of the socio-political processes of the society. In one aspect the modern state had and has to be very strong on dismantling certain structures and practices to enable the marginalized to emerge as respectable citizens and claim their entitlements. It is unfortunate that beyond enacting legislation and evolving policies, the State has not shown vigour in translating the legislations and the decisions into reality. Further in the Afro-Asian countries people do not understand the importance of representative democracy. Despite its being in practice for several decades, people do not understand the process of governance under representative democracy excepting 'voting'. As a result the governing mechanism superimposed on the society from above on the premise that if the State apparatus is expanded all developmental responsibilities will be handled effectively and that thereby society will be modernized and equity and equality will be achieved; by efficiently handling the State institutional mechanism economic development will be achieved through the western mode of production and the consequent development will be distributed equitably through the government institutions. The above premise has another underlying principle and assumption. That is the political institutions and State institutions will have the efficacy and efficiency to transform the society from backwardness to modernity. While evaluating the whole process of governance and development over a period of time it has been noticed that the avowed objectives have not been achieved through the structures created through the State apparatus. The State system has failed miserably.[3] The problems confronted in the formative years of establishment of governance after the departure of the colonial administration have continued to remain and new kinds of problems and issues have emerged due to the impact of modernization, industrialization and democratic governance through representative democracy. The countries which are facing severe crises in governance and development are in search of alternatives. The organisations and institutions which are working at the global level in development and governance have also analyzed the problems with the objective of finding out an institutional mechanism suitable to the ethos of the society and a suitable methodology for development. It is now widely accepted that pluralistic and widespread governance will be effective in managing the affairs of the society and hence authority and power should be spread at different levels and multiple centres of power have to be established.[4] Further the democratically elected governments have to be further deepened through decentralisation of powers.[5] Thus people have to be empowered to tide over the problems in governance. In this strenuous journey it is found that each and every society has its own institutional mechanism evolved over a period of time to manage its own affairs and they are dormant since the State apparatus has extended its tentacles to the grassroots as development bureaucracy and street bureaucracy work for development as per the direction of the government from above. Though they are dormant, they are having control over the community in performing certain minimal functions and hence they try to influence the State institutional mechanism to act according to their wishes.

As a result, the government, through its policies, programmes and schemes could not achieve the planned target. So micro institutional structures working at grassroots were identified as effective and feasible. To achieve local development and to achieve social reconstruction to address the issues of social justice, local institutions are considered appropriate. This was the new premise found out throughout the world.[6] But the local institutions have to be reformed as they are traditional in character and not inclusive and gender sensitive. Hence it was planned to create local institutions to achieve development legitimately and to perform the functions of the local institutions evolved by the communities.[7] Such local self governance created by the modern governments has gained attention throughout the world.[8] Around eighty countries are seriously involved in creating an alternative paradigm of governance and development. This new initiative is the result of the failure of the big governments in delivering services and goods, because, in many of the developing countries, State systems became weak and hence could not manage the society for reform.

All over the world, local bodies are being given due recognition through various means to establish them as institutions of governance legitimately and well within the framework of constitutional governments. Brazil, Denmark, France, India, Italy, Japan and Sweden have given constitutional status to local governments. Australia and the United States of America have given due status in state or provincial constitutions. New Zealand, the United Kingdom and a large number of countries have enacted legislation to accord recognition to the grassroots institutions. China is an exception as it has accorded status only through an executive order. By doing so, the governance mechanism at the grassroots has been formalized and legitimized. Institutional structures are created everywhere.[9]

In India, the 73rd Amendment has been introduced and consequently the provincial governments have enacted conformity legislations. Elections have been conducted and representatives have been positioned. Since reservation was given, in the Amendment and in the State Act, women and Dalits were elected to different positions of rural local bodies. The whole process of activating grassroots democracy meets with stiff resistance from the communities in many places in India. The constitutionally created structures are allowed to function at the grassroots but not with the full participation of people. Community organisations are vibrant in involving the people in local activities. The problem starts from the election itself. In many places women and Dalits are allowed to contest in the election on conditions. But, after the election, they are not allowed to function as representatives of the people. If they are women, the males of their family handle power.[10] If they are Dalits, dominant community leaders handle power.[11] In some places the positions are auctioned openly by the leaders of the traditional Panchayats. In a few places a small group in the traditional Panchayat decides the individual to be the leader. In some places where the seats are reserved for Dalits, community leaders resist the election commission's attempt to conduct the election.[12] Indian society is not an equal society. It has got social inequality, economic inequality and discrimination in terms of gender and marginalization. Despite the fact that provisions are made for the marginalized groups to participate in governance through the Constitution, the leaders from among Dalits and women are not allowed to function.

For the first time in India, after Independence, the western model of democracy penetrates into the rural areas through the 73rd Amendment to the Constitution. Wherever the society is modernized and oriented in representatives democracy, women and Dalits are allowed contest in the election and they are being supported by the communities to carry out their duties and responsibilities. Wherever the society is modernized and not properly oriented in representative democracy, women and Dalits are allowed to contest in the election but not allowed to carry out their work. Wherever women and Dalit leaders are having leadership skill and understanding, they interface with the traditional structures and manage the institutions so as to deliver services and goods effectively to the satisfaction of the people. Wherever the women groups and Dalit groups are active and cohesive and have got orientation, however weak the women and Dalit elected leaders, they are being supported by the groups and they are made to function effectively. Wherever the women and Dalit leaders are weak and communities are also not supportive to the legitimate constitutional governing institutions, the traditional leaders assert themselves and control the constitutional institutions. Wherever the societies are not modernized and people are not oriented in representative democracy with a weak bureaucracy, traditional institutions never allow the constitutional institutions to take shape through election. These are some of the premises emerging from our experience with local governance in India.

After the conduct of the elections, women and Dalits are in position in the governance institution. To carry out the activities of the local institutions the leaders have to equip themselves by building their skill, capacity and capabilities. When they build the capacity and capability they can manage the institutions, mobilize the people for effective participation in governance and development, and interface with traditional institutions and Government institutions at a higher level.[13] Managing the local bodies is not a single man's or woman's show. It requires the support of the family, peers, political party, civil society, and community leaders. It is a skilful job by which synergy among different stakeholders can be achieved.

In many places even in a modernized society, traditional institutions still do look after the affairs of the community such as temples, community properties especially commons and more particularly water and local disputes. The traditional institutions have a valid framework of governance to manage the commons, conduct temple festivals and resolve minor disputes. They also operate a huge corpus fund.[14] Since there is an accepted and standard mechanism to operate a funds from the corpus fund in a transparent way the community reposes confidence in the leadership. While looking at the basic principles of these traditional structures one finds modern indicators of good governance, namely, accountability, responsiveness and transparency but not inclusion of gender and marginalized groups. In many places even the leadership is also on a rotation basis or on the basis of election. After the Tsunami in Nagapattinam District, many of the fisherfolk Panchayats have been democratized by which election was introduced and women were also included in the committee for governance.

Whenever the bureaucracy is effective, it interferes in the functioning of the traditional structures when the traditional structures disturb the normal functioning of the constitutional structures at the grassroots. Wherever there is synergy between the two, it plays a supportive role.[15] The traditional institutions which are vibrant in some places by their performance and credibility are able to bring the constitutional bodies under their fold for which the community is also supportive. By doing so, the corpus of the traditional structure is enhanced by using the commons of the constitutional institutions.

The people who are the major source of support to both institutions make a balanced act by extending support to both in many places, extending active support to traditional institutions and passive support to constitutional institutions. In some places where there is active social conflict and the affected people are the marginalized, they extend support to the constitutional Panchayat and discourage the traditional Panchayat. In a few places both are in action and intense conflict prevails between the two with the support of two groups supporting them. People know the roles of both institutions. If they feel both institutions are active and deliver services reasonably they extend support to both, because people are economically and politically rational. In the event of failure of the State structure in delivery of services, people have no option and hence whatever mechanism is available at grassroots has to be supported. Whenever the conflict is intense between the collectivities within a geographical area where the constitutional Panchayat is co-terminus with the traditional Panchayat, the civil society and media have to play an active role to expose the malady and seek the intervention of Government institutions. It has been demonstrated that local institutions are vibrant and capable of achieving local development[16] but, at the same time, local development should be on a equitable basis. To achieve this the constitutional institutions have to be strengthened. The search is on throughout the world to find ways and means of strengthening the constitutional institutions.

## Experiences in India

It is unequivocally clear from reports that women and Dalits have come to power at the grassroots. Really they have formed the critical mass. But the critical mass has to perform the critical function. To perform the critical function an array of steps are to be taken at different levels starting from the federal government to the local society in a variety of ways. The women and Dalit leaders have started their struggle and many of them are emerging as models in achieving development and social justice after surmounting all the barriers and obstacles.[17] Still many of them are in struggle and have not achieved any result. Capacity-building is being done by various training institutions, support structure is being created at different levels to extend handhold support to leaders who are in struggle. The media has been oriented to capture the success stories and the struggles of the marginalized leaders for effective intervention of the State authorities.[18] Political parties which are pro-grassroots-democracy periodically represent the problems of the leaders of the marginalized groups in the Provincial Legislative Assembly through their representatives. The women leaders and Dalit leaders who have deep commitment to social transformation and rural development have formed their own organisation to raise their voice. While looking at the process of strengthening the grassroots democracy, one cannot under estimate the positive elements of the traditional structures which cannot be achieved through the modern State structure. The negative aspects of the traditional structures can be eliminated through an effective synergization between the two. It has taken place in many areas in India.[19]

## Case Studies from Tamil Nadu

When four Gram Panchayats Keeripatti, Pappapatti and Nattarmangalam of Madurai District and Kottakatchienthal in

Virudhunagar District were not allowed to have Dalit leadership it was effectively tackled by the District Administration. The whole State machinery helped to conduct the election by undermining the traditional structures. It is the best example to demonstrate how the State structures effectively intervened and restored democracy for inclusion. When *sati* was practiced in Madhya Pradesh, the Government fixed the responsibility on the constitutional Panchayats and stopped the development grants to the Panchayats by which *sati* was eradicated effectively through the constitutional Panchayats. While protecting the commons from the encroachment of the influential leader of caste and party, Urapakkam Gram Panchayat leader Ms.Menaka gave her life by which she created awareness among the people about the importance of natural resources.[20]

The President of K. Rayawaram Gram Panchayat in Pudukkottai District, Mrs. Rani Sathappan, accommodated the traditional Panchayat in the fold of the constitutional Panchayat and delivered services effectively for about ten years and won several awards for her outstanding performance. She ably demonstrated her leadership in managing the traditional Panchayat. Even the traditional Panchayat leaders appreciated the effective Performance of the woman leader.[21] She shared with the traditional Panchayat many of the responsibilities in the best interests of the community and the traditional Panchayat ably fulfilled all its responsibilities. Thus one can find synergy between the two structures.

Nattukottai Gram Panchayat in Sivaganga District was headed by a traditional Panchayat leader Mr.Ramanathan who has emerged as an outstanding leader in achieving infrastructure, development and social justice. He was the President of both the structures and worked for social justice and got several awards.[22] He held the position for several decades. In the absence of the constitutional Panchayat he carried out all the welfare activities in the village through the Government departments. He continued to be the traditional Panchayat leader. It is very vibrant in this Panchayat. A cultured and well oriented leader, he is sensitive to social justice and so worked for social equity and equality. It is to be noted that this district is known for conflict between traditional Panchayats and constitutional Panchayats as traditional Panchayats practice untouchability. But this Panchayat emerged as a model for social justice due to his leadership.

The Maravamangalam Gram Panchayat leader Mr.Annadurai was very popular among all segments of the society and got the support of all for all his transparent development activities. He used to keep the traditional Panchayat within the fold of the constitutional Panchayat. By doing so he succeeded in all his attempts.[23] It is to be noted that he belongs to the Communist Party of India. Normally the left parties are against the functioning of the traditional structures. Despite the poor presence of left party supporters in this village he was elected President because of the support extended by the community through the traditional structure. He worked hard to achieve social justice for which there was no resistance from the traditional structure. Hence he worked comfortably with the traditional Panchayat.

Noothulapuram Gram Panchayat President Ms. Kala, a Dalit woman, carefully developed a design to work effectively for the betterment of the Dalits by aligning with the traditional Panchayat leaders. The Dalits called it a compromise but she called it a strategy. According to her, one can be in struggle if suppression of the Dalits happens. But, to achieve development for a marginalized section, aligning with the traditional Panchayat is not a bad formula.[24] She argued that for her victory in the election, the traditional leaders also worked. When they were not against any development work for the Dalits why should one develop an antagonistic attitude towards the traditional leaders?

Kuthampakkam Gram Panchayat President Mr. Elango, by his extraordinary leadership qualities, fought with the bureaucracy and made the Panchayat a self governing institution. By his performance he transformed the entire village and more specifically the Dalits. He is a model for other Dalit Gram Panchayat leaders.[25]

His leadership is accepted by the community as he has demonstrated his leadership.

Ms. Pappa, President of Atthankaraipatti Gram Panchayat, formed a Dalit Women Federation to help the other Dalit Women leaders. She relentlessly waged a struggle against the political party leaders of that area. She succeeded in all her attempts. Thus the leaders of constitutional Panchayats have successfully transformed the development politics at the micro-level with different strategies.[26] Madurai, Sivaganga and Virudhunagar and some of the southern districts are known for the practice of untouchability and the strong presence of traditional community structures. Many reports both from research institutions and civil society organisations reveal that the constitutional Panchayats headed by Dalits are not allowed to function independently. But the cases explained above are mostly from the above districts. How were they able to succeed? It was because of the extraordinary leadership of the individuals. The leadership plays an important role in transforming institutions and society.

It has been demonstrated that the State structure as well as the traditional structure have strengths and weaknesses in terms of delivering services and achieving equity. In the absence of a vibrant local democratic mechanism, the traditional structures keep the people intact with them.

The traditional structures can be weakened by the effective performance of the State structures even at the local level. In the absence of such strong and vibrant State structures the traditional structure will maintain its primacy. In terms of leadership, the traditional leaders are known for their integrity, honesty and rectitude in handling finance and delivering services. Acceptable norms have been evolved over a period of time with the participation of the members of the community. Hence it is all known to the people whereas the western model of governance is not known to the people. The local governance institutions created through the Central and Provincial Governments have to imbibe the nature and character of the traditional institutions after eliminating the negative features of the traditional institutions.

## Conclusion

Constitutional institutions created at the grassroots should be made vibrant and they have to shed their present character of unresponsiveness to the demands of the people. A constant drive should be maintained from the upper level governments to strengthen the constitutional structures for which mobilization of the people is imperative. The elected leaders have to be equipped to carry out the roles and responsibilities of the grassroots institutions. Equally the traditional institutions have to be democratized and they are to be integrated with constitutional Panchayats. A meaningful synergy between the constitutional structures and the traditional structures will produce needed results from the grassroots institutions.

## NOTES

1. The following works reveal the potentials of the Grassroots institutions created through the historic amendments:
   Niraja Gopal Jayal, Amit Prakash and Pradeep K Sharma (eds) *Local Governance in India: Decentralisation and Beyond*, New Delhi: Oxford University Press, 2006; L.C. Jain (ed) *Decentralization and Local Governance*, New Delhi: Orient Tong Man, 2005; Girish Kumar, *Local Democracy in India: Interpreting Decentralization*, New Delhi: Sage Publications, 2006; and G.Palanithurai (ed), *Dynamics of New Panchayati Raj Systems in India*, New Delhi: Concept Publishing Company, 2004, Vol I, II & III.
2. G. Palanithurai, *Process and Performance of Women and Dalit Leaders*, New Delhi: Concept Publishing Company, 2004.
3. Bidyut Chakraparthy and Mohit Bhattacharya (eds), *Administrative Change and Innovation, A Reader*, New Delhi: Oxford University Press, 2005.
4. L.Hooghe and G.Marks, "Unravelling the Central-State, but How? Types of Multi-Level Governance", *American Political Science Review* 97:2 (2003) pp. 233-43.

5. Samuel P. Huntington, *The Third Wave: Democratization in the Late Twentieth Century* Norma: University of Oklahoma Press, 1991.
6. James Manor, *The Political Economy of Democratic Decentralisation*, Washington DC: World Bank, 1999.
7. George Lutz and Wolf Linder, *Traditional Structures in Local Governance for Local Government*, (Report of a Project Commissioned by the World Bank), Bern: Institute of Political Science, 2004.
8. Warren Magnusson, "Protecting the Rights of Local Self Government", *Canadian Journal of Political Science*, Vol.38 : No.4 (Dec, 2005) pp.897-922.
9. Warren Magnusson, Opcit,
10. G.Palanithurai, *Empowerment of Women: Problems Faced by the Elected Women Representatives* (Monograph), Gandhigram: Rajiv Gandhi Chair for Panchayati Raj Studies, 2001.
11. G.Palanithurai, *Dalit Leadership in Panchayats* (Monograph), Gandhigram: Rajiv Gandhi Chair for Panchayati Raj Studies, 2003.
12. G.Palanithurai, *Third General Election to Local Governments in Tamil Nadu: Expectations and Shocking Realities*, New Delhi: Concept Publishing Company, 2007.
13. G.Palanithurai, *Experience of Training and Capacity-Building of Local Body Leaders*, New Delhi: Concept Publishing Company, 2007.
14. V.Ragupathy, *Participatory Management of Natural Resources*, New Delhi: Concept Publishing Company, 2003.
15. G.Palanithurai, *Synergization of Traditional Panchayats with Formal Panchayati Raj System in Managing Community Affairs*, Gandhigram: Rajiv Gandhi Chair for Panchayati Raj Studies, 2003.
16. Hari Mohan Mathur, *Administering Development in the Third World: Constraints and Choices in the Third World*, New Delhi: Sage Publication, 1986.
17. G.Palanithurai, *Change Makers at Grassroots Democracy*, New Delhi: Concept Publishing Company, 2007.
18. G.Palanithurai, *Media and Grassroots Governance* (Monograph), Gandhigram: Rajiv Gandhi Chair for Panchayati Raj Studies, 2004.
19. Kripa Ananthpur, *Interfaces in Local Governance: A Study in Karnataka*, Chennai: MIDS, 2004 (Working Paper, 187); Kirpa Ananthpur, *Rivalry or Synergy? Formal and Informal Local Governance in Rural India* (Working Paper, 226), Sussex: IDS, 2004.
20. The Tamil Nadu Federation of Women Presidents, *Voices of Women Presidents of Panchayat Governments in Tamil Nadu*, Chennai: Human Rights Advocacy and Research Foundation, 2004.

21. G.Palanithurai, *Leadership Matters at Grassroots Governance: Path Finders Series IV, K.Rayavaram* (Monograph), Gandhigram: Rajiv Gandhi Chair for Panchayati Raj Studies, 2004.
22. G.Palanithurai, *Leadership Matters at Grassroots Governance: Path Finders Series VI, Nallukottai* (Monograph), Gandhigram: Rajiv Gandhi Chair for Panchayati Raj Studies, 2004.
23. G.Palanithurai, *Leadership Matters at Grassroots Governance: Path Finders Series XIII Maravamangalam* (Monograph), Gandhigram: Rajiv Gandhi Chair for Panchayati Raj Studies, 2005.
24. G.Palanithurai, *Leadership Matters at Grassroots Governance: Path Finders Series XXII, Noothulapuram* (Monograph), Gandhigram: Rajiv Gandhi Chair for Panchayati Raj Studies, 2006.
25. G.Palanithurai, *Leadership Matters at Grassroots Governance: Path Finders Series V, Koothampakkam* (Monograph), Gandhigram: Rajiv Gandhi Chair for Panchayati Raj Studies, 2004.
26. G.Palanithurai, *Leadership Matters at Grassroots Governance: Path Finders Series XXIII, Aathankaraipatti* (Monograph), Gandhigram: Rajiv Gandhi Chair for Panchayati Raj Studies, 2004.

# 3

# Synergization of Traditional Panchayat with Formal Panchayati Raj System in Managing the Community Affairs

*G.Palanithurai*

## Introduction

The 73rd Amendment to the Constitution of India has created space for decision-making by involving all social groups at the grassroots in the rural areas. This new dispensation has been imposed on communities which had their own structural arrangements to manage their community affairs by following the norms evolved over a period of time by the elite of the society, which is characterized as feudal, elitist, patriarchical and caste based and unchallenged (Lele, 2001). When the new formal institutions, with their earmarked responsibilities and powers, started functioning in the rural areas, they were confronted by the traditional Panchayats (Palanithurai, 2001). Wherever the traditional Panchayat is weak, the formal Panchayat establishes its sway and wherever it is strong the formal Panchayat cannot make inroads and, as a result, conflicts between the two Panchayats are visible. In Tamil Nadu, due to the Dravidian movement, the caste hierarchy had been diluted to some extent to the advantage of the backward classes (Indhu Rajagopal, 1985) but not to that of the Dalits. Wherever the Dravidian movement established its impact the traditional structure has been weakened. In the same way wherever the left movement registered an impact, the caste hierarchy has been dismantled even up to the Dalits and discriminatory practices have been mitigated if not eradicated*. This, however, is not uniform in all areas in Tamil Nadu. There are a few places where a synergy between the traditional Panchayat and the formal Panchayat has enabled the formal Panchayat to perform very well. Karisalpatti, a Gram Panchayat in Dindigul District, secured the second prize in Tamil Nadu State and the first prize at the district level to draw the attention of all as it performed well by synergising the two Panchayats.

## The Problem

This study makes an attempt to analyze the dynamics of the systemic fusion of the two Panchayats for the effective delivery of services to the people and to maintain harmony among the people in this Panchayat area. Before investigating the problem, it is necessary to take a look at the backdrop of the problem.

How power relations in the rural areas are to be analysed is a major area of focus for academics in Anthropology. Political scientists focus much attention on State politics and federal polity but rarely touch upon the formal Panchayat system under the caption of administration. Power and authority are vested with communities and community leaders to take decision which affect the life of the people. As power relationship changes at a snail's pace, it cannot be matched with the village economy and the state politics in terms of quantum of change. Power relations vary from place to place and region to region.

Studies on communities are available in plenty on the aspects of economy (Mukherjee, 1959), social structure and conflict of village communities (Basu and Kohli, 1998). But little attention has been paid to the power relationship between groups and communities in the villages (Andre Beteille, 1965) on the assumption that the communities are far from the power

* In certain districts, namely Nagapattinam and Thiruvarur in Tamil Nadu, the discriminatory practices have been totally eradicated.

relationship and operate outside the purview of State and Central politics. Though village dynamics are different and distinct, there are linkages between the village and the wider political system. These linkages are intensive only during the time of elections. Yet power relations are strong on deciding things which affect the life of the community. The political process can be examined from the perspective of the relationship between the formal Panchayats and the local elite, popularly called *grama nattanmai*. The formal Panchayats are vested with specific political functions and they are to play an influencing role in deciding things which affect the life of the people. At the same time the *grama nattanmai*, with his own council, has got legitimacy from the community to decide things in the community either in the presence of the formal Panchayat or in its absence. No matter what quantum of power the formal Panchayat enjoys, the traditional Panchayat has established its grip on the society. The manner in which power is distributed leads to the division of the village community into different categories. There are hierarchical arrangements in the traditional system. The traditional Panchayat has its own role in the electoral process of the formation of the formal Panchayat. Sometimes the role of the traditional Panchayat is vital in determining the victory of the candidates and sometimes the role of external political influence, particularly from the State politics, is vital in determining the victory of the candidates in the elections.

In the context of shifting power relations how the formal Panchayat manages the affairs of the community while facing the traditional Panchayat and the problems of the people is the major area of concern in this work.

## Methodology

To study the power dynamics in Karisalpatti Village Panchayat, the formal Panchayat leaders, the traditional Panchayat leaders and the Panchayat functionaries were contacted with the objective of eliciting their opinion of the success of the formal Panchayat in the context of the presence of traditional Panchayat. Formal

Panchayat leaders, informal community leaders and leaders of social and cultural institutions were asked questions relating to the success of the Panchayat. Their reactions and observations are presented in this work.

## History of the Village

Karisalpatti Gram Panchayat is a multi-caste village Panchayat situated on the northern side of the Kannivadi Hills which is a part of the Western Ghats range. Karisalpatti is the main village and along with it there are two hamlets, namely Pazhaya Kannivadi and Karamadai. Karamadai is a new habitation coming up on the Palani-Sempatti State Highway.

Christian Vanniars are the dominant caste group in this Panchayat. There are Hindu Vanniar families also living in the Panchayat area. It is stated that the Vanniars of this area had their origin in the Chozha kingdom. The present Thiruchirapalli was once under the Chozha kingdom. A zamindar in the Chola kingdom ruled over a small area around Lalgudi. The above said Vanniar community lived in the Lalgudi area. Once the zamindar went out for hunting, he commanded the Vanniar community men who accompanied him to carry his shoes when he had to cross a river. The Vanniar menfolk took it as an insult to the community and refused to do so and started a dispute with the zamindar and in the ensuring encounter the zamindar was killed. Fearing the wrath of the zamindari administration, the majority of the Vanniar families escaped from the Lalgudi area and proceeded south to seek a new habitation for their settlement. In this way their kith and kin settled here in Dindigul District. It was stated by the old men and women of this village that this incident occurred in the fifteenth century and that during the British period most of them converted to Christianity.

The Vanniars on the hillocks of Kannivadi are brave enough to domesticate wild elephants. The word *kari* means elephant and the word *patti* means shed (Cre-A, 1991). Karisalpatti is the place where the wild elephants are domesticated by the brave Vanniar community. The community has lived cooperatively and faced the elephant menace successfully. Hence the village is called Karisalpatti.

## Caste and Religious Composition

Christian Vanniars are the dominant caste group. There are 500 families belonging to the Christian Vanniar Community. The Hindu Vellalars are the next in numerical strength, with 150 families. People belonging to the SC number about 100 families. They are of the Parayar sub-caste. Chettiyars are a minority community and there are only ten families in Karisalpatti village.

Christianity is the main religion practised by 70 per cents of the population. Karisalpatti has been a Christian Parish since 1976. A primary school started in the year 1885 is run by the Parish. Now it is functioning with eleven teachers and four hundred students. To cater to the educational needs of the higher class students, in the year 1960, a high school was sanctioned to Karisalpatti at the initiative of the community leaders. The Karisalpatti Village community donated four acres of land and Rs.10,000 cash for starting the high school.

Religious celebrations by the Christian families bring about a feeling of oneness among them. There are seven Crusadies, that is, places earmarked for the fixing of the Holy Cross in seven streets. The families living in each street organize flag hoisting during festivals and distribute free meal to all. A car procession is also an event during the celebration. These religious activities make the people work together. The Parish priest exercises a moral authority over every Christian family. From birth till death a number of ceremonies have to be observed with the help of the Parish priest as done by the Hindus with the help of a Brahmin priest.

These Holy Sacraments create a sense of oneness among the Christians and create a conducive environment for undertaking any activities benefiting the community under the moral authority of the Parish priest. The Parish priest further explained that the sermons delivered by the Church authorities during the ceremony of the Mass includes guidance for day-to-day life also. The Church involves itself in creating awareness among the people about the importance of sanitation, childcare, women's development and public health.

## Role of Traditional Heads

When the Parish priest explained the social dynamics of the Christian community in Karisalpatti, he brought to light the power and authority of the traditional Panchayat leaders and their committees. In spite of the moral supremacy of the Parish priest over the Christian community, the Parish administration has to adjust with the traditional community system in Karisalpatti village.

The traditional Panchayat committee consists of three members. The *Nattanmai* is the head and the *Maniam* and the *Chinna Nattanmai* are his deputies. For any social activity or religious activity, the traditional Panchayat committee has to be consulted. This system has further cemented the solidarity among the communities. In villages traditional Panchayat committee members are mostly drawn from a set of families. It is observed that through the traditional Panchayat committee social control is imposed on the people of Karisalpatti. But the people of this area view this control as moral in nature.

Community mobilization among the Hindus is also being done through temples. Among the Hindu families caste-wise traditional committees are also functioning. Any dispute not settled by them is brought to the notice of the traditional Panchayat committee of the Christian Vanniars as it is the supreme body. The judgment delivered by this committee over the dispute between the members of other castes is final and accepted in general by all. Any violation or breach is treated as an anti-social activity. The first respect is always given to the traditional committee of the respective castes. At the same time the Christian Vanniars' Panchayat committee is considered supreme. It is said that the participation of women is generally not permitted during the meeting of the traditional Panchayat.

There are specific places earmarked for each caste where the traditional committee or any other common meet is organized. The village ground is earmarked for the Christian Vanniars, the temple campus for Vellalars, the Chavadi for Hindu Vanniars and the Dalit community has a separate place. People celebrate religious functions and spend a lot.

Collecting donations, planning of celebrations and organizing of various events by Hindus and Christians, though done separately, generates much socialization among the villagers. Both religious groups mutually admire and participate in the religious functions. Hence it is said that inter-caste and inter-religious marriages are common in Karisalpatti Village. There is no conflict among the caste and religious groups due to these inter-caste marriages since these marriages are accepted by the traditional Panchayat.

## Consolidation of Womenfolk

Harmony in a society can be easily disturbed if there is any conflict involving women in the rural areas. Women in general have been less oriented in social life. Now the trend is getting changed slowly. Activities relating to mobilizing women, initiated by the Church authorities as well as Government departments, have brought about a new climate in rural areas. Self-help Groups have brought together women of different communities. Though they deal among themselves in micro-credit and micro-finance activities, a number of other social activities are introduced to them. Awareness has been created among the women on education, health, sanitation, reproductive and child health and child welfare along with economic activities. There are five vibrant Self-help Groups working in Karisalpatti. With the help of an NGO the Self-help Groups got loan for their micro-finance activities. In addition to the above mentioned women related activities, nurses from the Christian Convent used to meet the womenfolk periodically and offer counsel to them. Awareness about health is being created by the nuns of the Convent where the nurse trainees used to go for their training placement. Yet the women have little role in the traditional Panchayat system.

## Youth and the Community

There is a Youth Committee constituted by the formal Panchayat for promoting sports and games. The youth of all castes are making use of this forum. In the name of V.O.Chidambaram (a freedom fighter), the youth belonging to the Vellalar community formed a group and the SC youth formed an Ambedkar Youth Association. The Christian youth have formed a Youth Club to undertake religious activities. Both religious and sports activities have brought the youth of different castes together. They stage dramas and cultural programmes during Christmas. The youth of Karisalpatti sustain the harmonious relationship among themselves and so far they have never entertained any ill will or hatered in the name of religion or caste. The community leaders never misguide the youth. Hence a smooth and congenial atmosphere prevails among the youth of Karisalpatti. Both the formal and traditional Panchayat leaders orient the youth properly for maintaining peace and communal harmony.

## Common Property Resources

### *(a) Drinking Water Resources*

There are five wells meant for drinking water, of which three are in use and the other two are not in use as the water in the wells has dried up. The drinking water has been brought under the comprehensive village water supply scheme of the Government. It is meant for two village Panchayats, namely Karisalpatti and Kasavanampatti. The sharing ratio of water between these two panchayat is 5:3. There are two overhead tanks and one ground level reservoir to supply water to 39 public taps and 130 individual taps in individual houses. A deposit of Rs.1000 each for all the 130 individual tap connections has been collected by the Panchayat. The monthly water tax of Rs.30 per household is also collected regularly. Cent per cent water charges collection has been ensured till July 2002. There are five handpumps, of which four are functioning well. In one bore well, a mini pump has been fitted with the financial assistance of TWAD. The village community cooperates in the maintenance of water supply points. In all collective action, the traditional Panchayat helps the formal Panchayat.

During the current season of severe drought due to the failure of the monsoon, in consultation with the community, a system of public water supply at one point was arranged for the continuous and equal distribution of water to all. In the meantime, the deepening of a well meant for drinking water was undertaken by the Panchayat. In the midst of a financial crisis, the Panchayat decided to draw money from the deposit money collected for individual tap connections. The President informed that the decision was intimated to the higher officials of the Department and, after the receipt of the grant from the Government, the money would be repaid to the water supply account. This decision of withdrawing of money is contrary to Panchayat rules. Yet, because the community insisted, the Panchayat took such a decision. The members unanimously resolved in this regard and if any action was initiated against the Panchayat, the village community as a whole would stand up to rescue the Panchayat. Being transparent in his transactions, the President commands respect and confidence and support among the public. The President said that a local youth could be given training in handpump mechanism by which means the dependence on the Panchayat union mechanic could be avoided.

### *(b) Streetlight Maintenance*

There are seventy seven tubelights in Karisalpatti. Sodium vapour lamps are not fitted anywhere in Karisalpatti. Though the Government of Tamil Nadu allowed the Panchayats to purchase sodium vapour lamps, the Karisalpatti Panchayat President declined to do so as it would increase the electricity bill. This decision was taken after consulting all concerned. The traditional Panchayat leaders are aware of the implications of the excess use of electricity and water and hence they always support the energy conservation activities. To them natural resources are the lifeline of the community. Now, when all Panchayats are facing financial crunch,

Karisalpatti maintains its finances very well. Maintenance work is carried out properly by the Panchayat. A ceiling of Rs. 22,000 is fixed for the head streetlights maintenance. The Gram Panchayat has never spent more than Rs.15,000. The Panchayat used to switch on the lights from 7.00 pm to 5.30 am only. The Village Panchayat is remitting the EB bill regularly and the community has extended their cooperation in the maintenance of streetlights.

### (c) Maintenance of Graveyard

There are five locations earmarked for graveyard. The extent of the site is as follows: 1 acre, 0.30 cent, 0.10 cent, 0.15 cent, and 0.05 cent. The approach roads to two sites were improved by the Panchayat. Half a kilometre of Black Top road and half a kilometre of mud road were laid. With the support of the community, a shed at a cost of Rs.15,000 was erected in the graveyard meant for the Christian community. When the demand for the provision of the shed came during the Gram Sabha, the Panchayat explained its inability but agreed to undertake road improvement. Hence the community happily came forward to meet the expenditure of the erection of a shed for funerals. In each and every activity of the formal Panchayat, the traditional Panchayat takes responsibilities including contribution in monetary terms.

### (d) Road Maintenance

The Gram Sabha decided which roads were to be converted to cement concrete. The village community listed six roads as having priority. Further the community decided to lay a BT road to the high school. Normally decisions are taken only after a prolonged discussion. On most occasions, the President used to take time to explain and convince the members and then only decisions are taken. People are oriented by the traditional Panchayat in participating in the meetings of the community. In the community meetings all the participants have equal opportunity to speak. The same practice has been extended to the Gram Sabha also.

### *(e) Community Tanks and Maintenance*

A tank under the category of Manthai remained unutilized for several years. When water was available, villagers used to take their cattle there. During 1997/98 the tank was desilted and deepened properly by the Panchayat after a decision was taken in the Gram Sabha meeting to augment resources through tree-plantation on the banks of the tank.

The Manthaikulam, with an extent of 2 acres, is now maintained properly. Seventeen coconut trees, 50 silk cotton trees, 50 bamboo trees, 50 tamarind trees and 10 vaagai trees have been planted on the banks of the tank. Before the growth of the trees an inter crop was proposed by the community and flower plants were cultivated. In the next two years Rs.10,000 was earned through the auction of these flower plants by the Panchayat. The community cooperated with the Panchayat in the maintenance of this tank. Fencing was done by the Panchayat. The youth helped to protect the tank. After the successful venture in the Manthaikulam, it was decided to undertake the planting of 400 silk cotton trees in another tank known as Kanakkankulam, which is four acres in extent. Three years after plantation, the silk cotton trees would yield Rs.10,000 per year. The maintenance of these tanks is possible for the Panchayat as the villagers have witnessed the utility of the common properties under the management of the Village Panchayat. Moreover any encroachment is dealt with seriously by the Panchayat irrespective of the community of the encroachers.

In many Gram Panchayats in Tamil Nadu eviction of encroachers is a tough job and the Panchayat leaders find it very difficult as the community leaders do not extend any cooperation. But in Karisalpatti the traditional Panchayat leaders help the Panchayat to retrieve the property from the encroachers.

### *(f) Maintenance of Orchards and Social Forestry*

The campus of the Village Panchayat office is vast. When the Gandhigram Rural Institute students proposed their camp in Karisalpatti, a village meeting was held to discuss the plan for utilising their camp days fruitfully. In that meeting a proposal was made to lay a garden in the campus. It was said that the plants could be irrigated as drain water is available from the nearby community hall. During 1998-99, the students' camp was organised. The village youth joined hands with farmers and reclaimed the land lying waste for many years. Now, a garden of nearly sixty banana trees, fifty coconut trees and six tamarind trees has come up in the campus. Marriages are conducted in the nearby community hall. For each marriage banana trees are needed as they are considered an auspicious welcome festoon. Hence, at the rate of Rs.75 each, banana trees are sold to the public. Since 1998-99 Rs. 9000 has been credited to the Panchayat account from the sale of banana trees.

### *(g) Claim over the Entitlement to Tamarind Trees*

The Sempatti-Palani State Rural Highway runs through Karisalpatti and Dharmathupatti villages. Each village Panchayat is a separate one but under the jurisdiction of one revenue village. So far the roadside tamarind trees were under the enjoyment of Dharmathupatti even though the rural highway runs through Karisalpatti Village Panchayat limits. When the Panchayat approached the Highways authorities to hand over the tamarind trees of Karisalpatti they asked to prove the entitlement of Karisalpatti. Hence the revenue authorities were contacted and, after duly verifying the survey number of the highway, the Village Administrative Officer certified that the land came under Karisalpatti Village Panchayat. It was found that there are 6 tamarind trees within the Karisalpatti Panchayat limits. Now, after paying the prescribed fees to the Highways, the Panchayat of Karisalpatti has got six tamarind trees. The village elders helped by accompanying the Panchayat President to meet the Highways officials. The village community's level of consciousness and interest in common property resources is very high and it is an example of an organized community.

### *(h) The Categories of Common Buildings*

Apart from sites, trees, ponds, and tanks a number of buildings are also listed as common property resources of the Panchayat. A look at the list of items under the head buildings in the register maintained by the Panchayat will make the visitor wonder. There are different types of buildings, all put to proper use in Karisalpatti village and the maintenance of these buildings is also taken care of by the Panchayat.

It is a common sight in any village that the public toilet is lying unused in spite of a pucca building constructed for the purpose. In Karisalpatti it is a different story. Two community toilets, one for males and the other for females, were constructed and both are used by the villagers. Awareness is created about the proper use and maintenance of these toilets by the Panchayat. Witnessing the successful use of the community toilets, an additional public toilet (a sanitary complex) was allotted and construction was completed. Women groups are entrusted with the responsibility of looking after these public toilets. Cards have been issued to the families and a nominal amount is collected for maintenance.

The Panchayat office building, the health sub-centre, the veterinary hospital and the community-cum-marriage hall are located in one campus. There are toilet facilities in the Panchayat office as well as the community hall. The toilet at the community hall was constructed from the incentive money given to Karisalpatti for the community's involvement through the Panchayat in the activities of a project on social development sponsored by population foundation of India. An old building was renovated and a part-time library is now functioning in it. The Annai Velankanni Pilgrimage Association donated folding chairs to the library. The villagers use this library. There are three TV rooms and the television sets are functioning well. The village volunteers are looking after these properties.

A ration shop is functioning in the Panchayat in its own

building. The maintenance of the same is also done whenever necessary by the Panchayat. There is a chavadi, a common place maintained by the Village Panchayat. The villagers make use of it as a place for rest and community meets. A balwadi is also functioning in an independent building owned by the Panchayat. There is a primary school run by the Panchayat Union. The maintenance work in the primary school is periodically done by the Panchayat. These common buildings are put to use effectively in Karisalpatti Panchayat. The Ward Members are asked to look after the buildings located in their respective wards. The youth are asked not to spoil the walls of these common properties. They help the Panchayat to maintain these buildings. Consciousness of the community in maintaining common properties is visible in Karisalpatti village as all buildings are in proper use.

## Community Initiative in Digging a New Tank

Due to scarcity of irrigation water the farmers of Karisalpatti felt very badly the unexpected fall in the level of their ground water sources. Understanding the importance and necessity of creation of a new water storage tank for their farm land, the farmers expressed their felt need for constructing a new tank in their area during the Gram Sabha meetings. The Panchayat President informed the community of the non-availability of any common land to spare for digging a new tank. Further, during the discussion on the subject, a few farmers suggested that there was a site of an extent of 4 acres owned by the Parish of Karisalpatti which could be the fittest site for the construction of a new tank. Its topography was suitable to serve as a catchment area and a channel was also running on the other side, which could be made use of for outlet of water if necessary during the monsoon. As the suggestion attracted all it was decided to make efforts under the leadership of the Panchayat to get the particular land from the Parish of Karisalpatti.

The Anthoniar Tank Renovation committee was constituted to take up this assignment. The President of Karisalpatti Village Panchayat served as advisor to the committee. There were eleven members in the Committee. Village elders, community leaders and farmers used to attend the meetings of this Committee.

The Committee met the Parish priest and the traditional Panchayat committee members and shared the idea of construction of a new tank for the benefit of the villagers in general and the farming community in particular. The factor of non-availability of any other common land was duly highlighted. After considering the plea of the villagers, the Parish came forward to spare the land of 4 acres. The value of the land was Rs.1.5 lakhs. The Church authorities permitted the villagers to dig a new tank there. The Committee appealed to all farmers whose lands were spread around the land earmarked for the tank to join in this endeavour. Though the property belonged to the Parish, cutting across religions, farmers of both Christian and Hindu religions contributed money. Rs.1.0 lakh was collected and digging was undertaken. The villagers requested the Panchayat to help in the construction of a check dam across the channel running along the tank. A resolution was passed in the Panchayat Council meeting and the District Panchayat was contacted for funds. At a cost of Rs.0.70 lakh the check dam cum outlet sluice arrangement was constructed.

Some individuals failed to appreciate the good efforts of the public. A few individuals reported to the higher authorities that the Panchayat misguided the District Panchayat and that the Village Panchayat showed the patta land as poramboke. Due to this complaint the allocation of funds was delayed. Then the records were verified and it was proved that the site identified for the check dam-cum-outlet sluice was of the category of odai poramboke as per the village revenue records. Hence an extent of 5 × 10 metre land was put to proper use where the check-dam was constructed. As a token of appreciation of the community the local member of the Legislative Assembly took part in the ceremony organised jointly by the Anthoniar Tank Renovation Committee and the Village Panchayat during 2001-2002. It is said that the Parish authorities consented to give in writing to the Anthoniar Tank Renovation Committee that the tank could be utilised by all the people though the Parish owns the legal title to the land. The important principle of local dynamics operated during the whole process of the dialogue between the Church and the Anthoniar Tank Renovation Committee. The Panchayat leaders clearly understood the local dynamics and so facilitated the interaction between the Tank Committee and the Church.

### The Status of Revenue Poramboke in Karisalpatti

There is a total extent of 15 hectares of poramboke land in the following categories:

| | | |
|---|---|---|
| Road poramboke | - | 5 hectares |
| Odai poramboke | - | 5 hectares |
| Natham poramboke | - | 5 hectares |

The Village Administrative Officer, when interviewed, informed that there is no land available in the Karisalpatti Panchayat limits for assignment, except the above rementioned road, odai and natham porambokes. Under natham poramboke, apart from the existing houses, the front yard of each house also comes under the natham account. Hence it could not be assigned to others as the households themselves kept these lands in their possession (Panchayat Records, 2001).

He suggested that memos under 'B' form, challenging any encroachment, should not be issued for the forest and hillside lands. These lands come under non-cessable land and so they could not be made available for assignment to any individual. But, at the same time, when 'B' memo is served, the encroacher used to take the issue to court and continue to enjoy these lands without paying any compensation to the Government. Moreover the encroachers of this type are usually not small farmers or landless labourers, but mostly rich and wealthy individuals. The VAO suggested to constitute a joint committee consisting of Panchayat, Forest, Revenue Officials and representatives of the general public to look after these common property resources for their proper maintenance, protection if need arises, for the distribution of these lands to the community or to individual beneficiaries. Now vast extents of non-cessable lands are under the clutches of rich people in the hillsides of Kannivadi. He maintained that if the Panchayat and Revenue administration joined together a more successful management of common property resources would be possible.

To generate additional income to the Panchayat, enhancement of house tax was proposed by the Ward Members during the Panchayat Council meeting. The proposal was discussed during the Gram Sabha meet held on 18th May 2002 and it was resolved to enhance the house tax slab from Rs.11 to Rs.22 and Rs.22 to Rs.33 and the licence fee collected from the shops was enhanced from Rs.50 to Rs.75. Further it was decided to increase the rent of the community hall from Rs.500 to Rs.750. These proposals did not cause any problem during the Gram Sabha meeting. The participants approved of the enhancement unanimously.

A deadline was fixed to collect the cable TV tax from the cable TV operator, and, after this, the cable TV operator paid the tax for 55 connections at the rate of Rs.10 per connection till April 2002. The operator promised to pay the balance tax amount at the earliest. The deposit of Rs.10,000 as per the Government Order has also not yet been paid by the operator. This was informed to the public during the Gram Sabha meeting.

## Milk Producers Cooperative Society *Vs* Panchayat

In Karisalpatti, the majority caste of Vanniars consolidated their unity through their caste association of Vanniar Sangam during the statewide mobilization-cum-movement initiatives under the leadership of Dr.Ramdass. It was reported that the State high command of the Vanniar Sangam misguided the Vanniars and instigated them to resort to violence. The Karisalpatti experience was otherwise. Of course the Vanniars of Karisalpatti too were sensitized and organized themselves like the Vanniars of other parts of the State during the movement. At the same time, they developed a positive mental attitude through this process. The Church played a predominant role in culturing the community rather than instigating the community to resort to violence. They organized a cooperative society for milk producers along with the caste organizational activities during the 1980s. In the year 1988, the

Karisalpatti Milk Producers' Cooperative was formed with 700 members. It is said that the society brought about a basic change in the lifestyle of the Vanniar community. The menfolk engaged in rearing milch animals and so they used their time and energy constructively. Otherwise they would have often engaged in disputes with others or among themselves and lost peace in their life. Rearing of milch animals became a full time job for those families who were landless and the landed gentry also spared their time and energy for this avocation as it was one of the allied activities of agriculture. The Milk Producers' Cooperative created an impact on the socio-economic life of each family in Karisalpatti.

The pioneers who formed the Society sustained their leadership in spite of the curse of political interference in the cooperative sector. The Society initially functioned well. But recently there have been maladministration and benami transactions. When credit facility was given to procure milch animals for the members, the President of the Society released loan amounts in the name of six members who were his kith and kin. Rs.1.70 lakh fell due from their account and in the meantime he sold all the milch animals also. Being a defaulter himself, the President could not command the other members when they failed to bring milk to the Society. The actual sufferers were those who regularly supplied milk to the Society. About Rs.5 lakhs, due to those who regularly supplied milk, could not be paid. After registering complaint with the District Registrar of Cooperatives, the members sold their milk to private vendors and they too started defaulting.

## Intervention of Panchayat

The President of Karisalpatti Panchayat happened to be the Vice-President of the Milk Society. All the members of the Society asked him to take necessary action against the culprit. A team of villagers and the Panchayat President met the concerned officials and the cheque power of the board of the Society was withdrawn so that further misappropriation could be prevented.

The traditional Panchayat meeting was convened and the

President of the Society being the *Chinna Nattanmai* of the community, the suggestions of the Panchayat President in this regard were accepted. The accused person sought one month's time to settle the loans and, with the witness of Police officials, time was given. But he failed to repay as promised and so an Action Committee was formed under the leadership of the Panchayat President. A proposal for road roko was announced. The Police and the Revenue Officials swung into action and they warned the accused that he would be arrested. He undertook to pay Rs.25,000 within 10 days and the balance amount within a month. He paid Rs.25,000 to the Society but he failed to pay the balance. Again the Committee announced an agitation and Rs.20,000 was paid by the accused. Time has been given to pay the balance.

The Panchayat President said that most of the members of the Society belong to the DMK Party, whereas he belongs to the AIADMK Party. But all of them unanimously resolved to make him the chairperson of the Action Committee. They repose faith in his leadership, not because of his party involvement, but because of his leadership in the Panchayat. The village community considers him their common leader. Thus the Panchayati Raj System has brought about a new trend in local leadership.

## Panchayat Income and Expenditure

House tax, professional tax, licence fees, building licence fee, rent from Panchayat buildings, auction of fish ponds and trees, entertainment tax, cable TV tax, advertisement tax, stamp duty share, land tax share and grants from Government are the major sources of revenue. The State Finance Commission grant, matching grant for house tax, grant for the funeral expenses of poor SC families and other grants are also received. On the expenditure side, the following items of expenditure are recurring ones and the expenditure can not be avoided as if the statutory responsibility of any Village Panchayat: salary to Panchayat staff, maintenance of roads and streets, maintenance of drinking water supply system, payment of electricity bills for streetlights, Panchayat buildings and water supply pumps, maintenance of streetlights, maintenance of environmental sanitation, sitting fee to Panchayat Ward Members, stationery and postage expenses and TA to the clerk and the President. Further the doles to Panchayat staff as per the Government direction have to be given by the Panchayat and all these items of expenditure have to be met from the income of the Village Panchayat.

Scheme funds allotted by both Centre and State can not be diverted to the above mentioned activities. The scheme funds have to be spent for the specified work as per the direction of the Central and State Governments. Most of the time the funds are tied up. Even the felt needs prioritized by the people could not be taken up under the scheme funds. In this context augmentation of the Panchayat's own resources becomes an urgent necessity. Karisalpatti Panchayat felt the need and took steps to improve its income sources through common property resources. A review of the income and expenditure of Karisalpatti since the introduction of the new Panchayati Raj System will give a lot of information on the efforts taken by the Panchayat in resource mobilization as well as activities initiated for the betterment of the public.

**Table 3.1 :** Income and Expenditure of the Panchayats during 1996-97

| Sl.No. Income | Rs. | Expenditure | Rs. |
|---|---|---|---|
| 1. Stamp Duty | 40918.00 | Maintenance of Water Supply | 2985.00 |
| 2. House & Professional Tax | 5884.00 | Salary of Staff and TA | 21397.00 |
| 3. Auctioning of Trees | 2350.00 | EB Charges | 24096.00 |
| 4. Matching Grant for House Tax Collection | 1012.00 | Streetlight Maintenance | 365.00 |
| 5. Opening Balance | 5667.00 | Closing Balance | 7753.00 |
| **Total** | **55831.00** | **Total** | **56596.00** |

*Source :* Computed from Karisalpatti Gram Panchayat records.

It is observed that 40 per cent was spent for establishment, 5.64 per cent for water and sanitation and 45 per cent for payment of electricity bills during the period 1996-97.

**Table 3.2 :** Income and Expenditure of the Panchayats during 1997-98

| Sl. No. Income | Rs. | Expenditure | Rs. |
|---|---|---|---|
| 1. House Tax | 4100.00 | Establishment | 37410.00 |
| 2. Professional Tax | 9900.00 | EB charges | 28811.00 |
| 3. SFC Grant | 53445.00 | Water and Sanitation | 13103.00 |
| 4. Other Grant (Matching Grant) | 24860.00 | Common Property Management | 3453.00 |
| | | Streetlight Maintenance | 4285.00 |
| | | Road Repair | 500.00 |
| | | Other Expenses | 1877.00 |
| | | Balance | 2788.00 |
| **Total** | **92305.00** | **Total** | **92227.00** |

*Source :* Computed from Karisalpatti Gram Panchayat records.

The expenditure during 1997-98 is observed to be 40.60 per cent for establishment, 31.27 per cent for electricity bills, 14.22 per cent for water and sanitation, 3.74 per cent for common property resource management and 4.65 per cent for streetlight maintenance.

**Table 3.3 :** Income and Expenditure of the Panchayats during 1998-99

| Sl. No. Income | Rs. | Expenditure | Rs. |
|---|---|---|---|
| 1. Comprehensive Water Supply Scheme | 26652.00 | Establishment | 54151.00 |
| 2. Auction of Flowers | 400.00 | EB Charges | 37885.00 |
| 3. Community Hall Rent | 750.00 | Water and Sanitation | 22269.00 |
| 4. Building Licence | 950.00 | Construction of new Buildings TV room | 48044.00 |
| 5. Stamp-Duty Share | 46373.00 | | |
| 6. House Tax matching Grant | 21864.00 | | |
| 7. SFC Grant | 53557.00 | | |
| **Total** | **150546** | **Total** | **162349** |

*Source :* Computed from Karisalpatti Gram Panchayat records.

There were many items of income during the year 1998-99. As house tax was increased the incentive given by the State Government also increased under house tax matching grant. Professional tax collection also increased. The drinking water supply was through a comprehensive rural water supply scheme which included another nearby Panchayat.

**Table 3.4 :** Income and Expenditure of the Panchayats during 1999-2000

| Sl. No. Income | Rs. | Expenditure | Rs. |
|---|---|---|---|
| 1. House Tax and Matching Grant | 34251.00 | EB Charges | 74808.00 |
| 2. Professional Tax | 16740.00 | Sanitation | 25534.00 |
| 3. Dangerous Objectional Trade Licence | 4260.00 | Maintenance of Streetlight and Drainage | 45559.00 |
| 4. Community Hall Rent | 9500.00 | Bank Balance | 9686.00 |
| 5. Tree Auction | 3919.00 | | |
| 6. Stamp-Duty Share | 34726.00 | | |
| 7. SFC Grant | 109034.00 | | |
| 8. Comprehensive Drinking Water Supply | 26485.00 | | |
| 9. Other Grants | 10586.00 | | |
| 10. Auction of Wastage and Scraps | 284.00 | | |
| **Total** | **249785.00** | **Total** | **155587** |

*Source :* Computed from Karisalpatti Gram Panchayat records

**Table 3.5 :** Income and Expenditure of the Panchayats during 2000-2001

| Sl. No. Income | Rs. | Expenditure | Rs. |
|---|---|---|---|
| 1. House Tax | 15900.00 | Establishment | 76221.00 |
| 2. Matching Grant | 15150.00 | EB charges | 72744.00 |
| 3. Professional Tax | 16150.00 | Sanitation | 32109.00 |
| 4. Building Licence | 3080.00 | Maintenance of Street Lights and other Properties | 67338.00 |
| 5. Income from Community Hall | 9250.00 | Purchase of Sports Materials | 2850.00 |
| 6. Income from common Properties, Trees and Flowers | 4938.00 | Bank Balance | 179661.00 |
| 7. Stamp-Duty Share | 44295.00 | | |
| 8. SFC | 81150.00 | | |
| 9. Comprehensive Water Supply Scheme | 15046.00 | | |
| 10. Award Money | 200000.00 | | |
| 11. GRI Grant | 8000.00 | | |
| **Total** | **412959.00** | **Total** | **430923** |

*Source :* Computed from Karisalpatti Gram Panchayat records.

## Scheme Funds

**Table 3.6 :** Receipt Details

| Sl. No | Year | Scheme | Amount (Rs.) |
|---|---|---|---|
| 1. | 1996-1997 | JVVT | 68,000 |
| 2. | 1997-1998 | JVVT | 50,692 |
| 3. | 1998-1999 | JVVT | 70,660 |
| 4. | 1999-2000 | JGSY | 51,623 |
| 5. | 2000-2001 | JGSY | 53,539 |
| 6. | 2001-2002 | JGSY 1st installment | 54,100 |

*Source :* Computed from Karisalpatti Gram Panchayat records.

## Activities Undertaken Under Scheme Funds

(a) Adi Dravidar colony improvement, TV room, Chavadi, Cement concrete roads, threshing floor, were provided at a total cost of Rs.92,105

(b) Culverts, retaining wall, kitchen room for community hall, drainage were provided at a cost of Rs.89,530.

(c) Community toilet for women, CRSP toilet, community toilet for men were constructed at a total cost of Rs.91,305.

(d) CC road was provided to main streets at a cost of Rs.16,104.

An allocation of Rs. 59,446 was made for the construction of a toilet in the SC colony. Due to inadequate space, the families did not want a toilet. Hence the amount was refunded.

From this analysis it is observed that, without tapping additional sources, the Village Panchayat cannot meet the recurring expenses under various items like establishment, payment of EB bills, water and sanitation expenses, maintenance of streetlights, roads, streets, buildings and other common property resources.

In Karisalpatti an attempt was made to generate additional income through growing trees in the Panchayat tank and Panchayat premises, claiming entitlement to roadside trees and improving the facilities in the community hall so that it could be rented for functions. Further, with the involvement of the community, the administration of the Panchayat was able to enhance the taxes, collect the taxes and avail of the matching grant from the Government. Moreover it got the award money of Rs.2.0 lakhs and Rs.8,000 from the Government and Gandhigram Rural Institute respectively for its good performance in carrying out its functions. This could be achieved only with the support and cooperation of the community. We can understand the synergization of the Village Panchayat with and the traditional Panchayat. It is understood that the Karisalpatti Village community realizes the significance of the power, authority and function of the Village Panchayat under the New Panchayati Raj System and so the community make proper use of the Panchayat for its development. And the Panchayat leadership understands the strength of the community and so gives due recognition to the community, duly holds consultation with the community, and, avails of its opinion and guidance whenever necessary for smooth and successful administration in the Panchayat.

## Conclusion

The New Panchayati Raj System was introduced with the twin objective of bringing about economic development in rural areas and ensuring social justice. Further, to strengthen the grassroots democracy, the participation of the people is encouraged through Gram Sabha meetings. The earlier system of Panchayati Raj did not provide for the involvement of the community and so a gap developed between the community and the Panchayat which destroyed the community initiatives through the Panchayat. These drawbacks have been removed in the new system. In Karisalpatti Village Panchayat, after the introduction of the New Panchayati Raj System, the leadership is capacitated and the community is informed well about the Panchayati Raj System. Stress is given to mobilizing the community through the Panchayat. Community based organizations are properly linked with the Panchayat. Against this backdrop this study has been made of the involvement of the community in the management of common property resources in

Karisalpatti through the Village Panchayat. The findings are as follow:

A capacitated Panchayat leadership comprehended the ways and means of development. Linkages with community-based organizations helped the Panchayat to strengthen its power and so delivery was qualitatively good. If common property resources could be improved, income to the Panchayat would be augmented in which the traditional Panchayat plays an important role. Special funds are needed to improve common property resources. Expenditure on establishment, EB bills and maintenance is always high. Prudent counsel provided by the traditional Panchayat helped the Panchayat to manage its finances. The Panchayat must be enabled to promote awareness on Panchayati Raj, sanitation and public health. Instead of tying up grants, the Panchayat should be permitted to make use of scheme funds for felt needs.

Mobilization of the community is the prerequisite for any developmental activities and it is not easy for the Government machinery to mobilize the people. The Village Panchayat, under the New Panchayati Raj System of governance, has ample opportunities to interact with the people for a better orientation of the community to plan and work for the better utilisation of common property resources. In circumstances wherein the traditional community understands the power and responsibility of the New Panchayati Raj Institutions the Panchayati Raj leadership should be proactive. The leadership of the traditional Panchayat and its strength have to be understood by the President and Ward Members of Panchayati Raj Institutions. It is expected that, for any development, pooling energies is required in the context of resources crunch as well as the erosion of democratic values in the Governmental system. The stakeholders could be mobilized for the better management of common property resources by the Panchayat if the Panchayat leadership is proactive and well-oriented in the art of managing the Panchayat. In the case of Karisalpatti, the President who served during 1996-2001 was Mr.Irudayam. He was the pioneer who organised the Annai

Velankanni Pilgrimage Association, one of the religion based community organizations in Karisalpatti. His proactive role in various public activities was observed by the community. His religious catholicism was appreciated even by people belonging to the Hindu community. Hence he won in the elections and successfully managed the Panchayat. The Government of Tamil Nadu, after evaluating the performance of Karisalpatti Panchayat, awarded the second prize at the State level and the first prize at the District level to Karisalpatti. Mr. Irudhayam got his training and intensive orientation through the Rajiv Gandhi Chair for Panchayati Raj Studies of Gandhigram Rural Institute.

For the next period of 2001-2006, Mr. Joseph Irudhayaraj @ Soodamani has been elected President. He is a traditional leader as he was a *Chinna Nattanmai* in the traditional committee of Christian Vanniars. Moreover he belongs to the AIADMK Party. He is an active member of that party. In spite of that he has ensured fairness in his administration.

It is a rare phenomenon that in Karisalpatti both the ex-President and the current President work together for the development of their village. The ex-President frequently visits the Panchayat office, helps in the day-to-day administration, accompanies the current President whenever necessary to various places in connection with public assignments and also gives encouragement to the President in the Panchayat administration. This rare phenomenon helps in the management of common property resources in Karisalpatti which motivated the present researchers to undertake a study of this process for dissemination.

## REFERENCES

A. Beteille, (1965). *Caste, Class and Power: Changing Patterns of Stratification in a Tanjure Village*, Berkeley: University of California Press.

Amrita Basu and Atul Kohli, (1998). *Community Conflicts and the State in India*, Delhi: Oxford University Press.

Cre-A, (1991). *Kriyavin Tarkalat Tamil Akarati* (Dictionary of Contemporary Tamil), Chennai: Cre-A. p. 661.

G.Palanithurai, (2001). *Problems Faced by the Leaders of Gram Panchayat*, Gandhigram: Rajiv Gandhi Chair for Panchayati Raj Studies.

Indhu Rajagopal, (1985). *The Tyranny of Caste*, New Delhi: Vikas.

Karisalpatti Panchayat, (2001). Panchayat Records.

M.K. Lele, (2001). "Local Government: Conflict of Interests and Issues of Legitimisation," *Economic and Political Weekly*, xxxvi:51 (Dec, 22) p. 4702.

P.K. Mukherjee, (1959). *Economic Survey in Under Developed Countries*, Bombay: Popular Prakashan.

# 4

# Role of Panchayats in Ground Water Management

*G.Palanithurai*

## Introduction

Conservation of natural resources was effectively done by the communities with the advice of local experts and by following community laws.

It is evident that the management of water resources was one of the responsibilities of the communities at the grassroots level ever since communities were recognized as responsible institutions for governance. There are arguments that the community organizations were quite effective in natural resource management and hence all over the world a search is on for reviving and reinventing the community organizations to take over such age old responsibilities of managing natural resources. It is also equally true that many of these community-based institutions have excluded many marginalized groups from the orbit of managing the natural resources. After the establishment of Nation-State system, the State assumed responsibilities from the traditional organizations. Yet the Government institutions neither enriched nor protected effectively the natural resources and hence they turned again toward community organizations. Over a period of time the modern State system, by its ruling character, has reduced the people to abject beneficiaries and petitioners. Despite the all-pervasive presence of Government, people strongly believe only in the community system and have retained the management of water bodies and temples with them. Water bodies are retained with the community as their livelihood depends on them. In the same way temples are retained with the communities as they are the pride of the communities. Tanks and temples were sacred to the community. Over a period of time the political institutions by their activities started breaking the local communities and communities lost their power over the natural resources and other community assets. As a result community assets have been neglected, abused and encroached upon.

To bring back the people to the process of governance and evolve a plan for the development of communities a new institutional mechanism has been created through the Constitution. The 73rd Amendment to the Constitution of India has provided enough scope for the people to evolve a micro-plan for each and every Gram Panchayat by which natural resources can be managed, infrastructure facilities created, and the created infrastructure facilities be utilized properly and productively. The plan should aim at achieving economic development and social justice.

In the 73rd Amendment there is a provision in the 11th Schedule for the Panchayats to deal with maintenance of community assets. A variety of activities related to water harvesting, water conservation, percolation and regulation of use of water can be planned and implemented by the Panchayati Raj Institutions. Out of the 29 items listed in the 11th Schedule of the Indian Constitution at least eight items are closely related to the use of water. They include minor irrigation, watershed development, water management, land improvement, soil conservation, minor forest, social forestry, drinking water, agriculture, and fisheries.

Many of the State Acts have given varied vital responsibilities related to conservation and management of water. In Tamil Nadu, maintenance of minor irrigation works like irrigation tanks, management of common lands, unreserved forests are entrusted to Panchayats. Most of the programmes of State and Central Governments related to water and land are implemented by the Panchayats. Programmes like the Rural Employment Guarantee Scheme have opened tremendous opportunities for Panchayats to work in the area of water harvesting and conservation.

They have also demonstrated that the available ground water can be used economically and equitably distributed. Panchayats have demonstrated that they can create a water culture at the grassroots. Many Panchayats have successfully improved ground water through rainwater harvesting, construction of checkdams, percolation ponds, desilting of water bodies and maintenance of supply channels. Like irrigation tanks ground water is also a common property. It is the responsibility of the State to regulate the use of ground water. But due to various reasons the State is not in a position to effectively implement regulatory measures to ensure economic and scientific use of ground water. Many of the acts and rules regarding regulating the use of ground water are hardly implemented. Water mining has become an industry and it is going on in the nooks and corners of the rural area and the State has very limited information on these activities. Due to urbanization, commercialization of agriculture, collapse of traditional institutions, land reform policies, the commons are under threat; particularly water bodies all over the country are under stress. Encroachment on water bodies is politically encouraged. A new water market has emerged and water is converted into a commodity. Free distribution of electricity for agriculture and commercialization of agriculture encouraged large scale use of ground water. Water lords have emerged in rural areas who control use of ground water. Over exploitation of ground water has resulted in the exclusion of marginal farmers from irrigation. Large scale rural indebtedness and suicide have been generated by over exploitation of ground water.

Panchayats have demonstrated that they could emerge as the guardians and custodians of water. In many parts of Tamil Nadu Village Panchayats have emerged as models for conservation of water and development of ground water. A variety of community based innovative strategies have been identified and used by them.

As per the Tamil Nadu Panchayati Raj System, the following activities have been entrusted to the Panchayats.

## Minor Irrigation

(1) Village Panchayats can assist the Panchayat Union to identify the tanks with ayacut area of less than 100 acres, and for the collection of information on water spread area, water holding capacity and period of storage to plan and execute necessary works.
(2) Taking appropriate action for desilting of tanks with an ayacut of less than 100 acres during summer season for increasing the water storage capacity of the tanks.
(3) The Village Panchayats may avail such benefits for reconstruction of supply channels of tanks with an ayacut of less than 100 acres and sinking of deep borewells.
(4) Assist in the identification of beneficiaries under Western Ghat Development Programme.

## Water Management

(1) The respective Village Panchayats can initiate action to collect details regarding the water table of their area from the Geologist and take suitable action.
(2) The Village Panchayats may take steps to search for the possibilities of sinking borewells for improving irrigation facilities in cultivable lands.
(3) The message of keeping adequate spacing between two open wells as per the opinion of the Geologist may be spread among the public.

## Watershed Development

(1) The Village Panchayats can assist in the compilation of details on land records, information on cultivable lands, pasture, wastelands, water harvesting structures, tanks bunds and other Panchayat lands and community asset, detect encroachments and evict such encroachment.

(2) Taking actions to implement all schemes under Watershed Development Programme should be the domain of Village Panchayats. In order to increase the production and proper usage of public land and other assets, Village Panchayats may supervise and take necessary actions. Coordinating with various departments for conservation of natural resources and protecting the ecology and environment.

(3) The Village Panchayats can prepare plan and implement the Watershed Development Programme in their areas. They can also identity the type of trees and plants which are suitable to the soil types.

(4) Village Panchayats can assist in the identification of beneficiaries under the Watershed Development Programme.

From the time of inception of the New Panchayati Raj System, activities earmarked under the subject 'Minor Irrigation' have been implemented by the Village Panchayats from the allocation of State and Central scheme fund. The Village Panchayat leaders, in course of time, after building their capacity to manage the affairs of the Panchayat, strengthened their vision in respect of common property resources—its protection and promotion and its better utilization. Especially the activities under ground water management are now slowly picking up as schemes like JRY, NREGA and DPAP very particularly demand the Village Panchayats to plan and execute the activities pertaining to augmenting ground water sources.

There are a large number of Gram Panchayat leaders sensitive on this issue and they have taken keen interest in mobilizing the people and have carried out a lot of activities in their respective Panchayats. Many of them are men, women and Dalits. They are committed and by using the limited powers devolved to them carry out activities. It is not so easy to carry out activities. They found out resources and carried out activities facing a volley of problems. Constantly they are in struggle. Yet after completing the activities and seeing the implications people started supporting the Panchayat leaders. A few cases are selected from Tamil Nadu for presentation. Following are the cases:

## Village Panchayats which are Emerging as Models

### *(1) Ms. Jesumary, President, Michael Pattinam Panchayat, Ramnad District*

Michael Pattinam is a very dry area. The people depend on rain to undertake farm activities. Only a few families posses wells. She explained to the people that the waterways should be cleaned before the rain comes and desilting of tanks has to be done. She also told them that desilting of tanks would help not only agricultural activities, but also their cattle. She convened the Gram Sabha meeting and explained to them about the conditions. The villagers worked overnight and they cleaned the waterways and strengthened the checkdams. It was a pleasant shock to the other Panchayat Presidents and officials including the District Collector. Everyone realized the potential of the community, and it was a breakthrough in her work, which has raised her image among the people. She is known throughout the State for her innovative rain water harvesting. She took pains to convince the people. She created a pucca rain water structure in all the streets of the village. She has been cited in the letter written by the then Chief Minister J.Jayalalitha to Panchayat leaders. She is a pioneer in rain water harvesting. She was invited to Washington by the World Bank. She got several awards. Further she constructed several checkdams in her Panchayat area despite opposition from other villages.

### *(2) Ms. Rani Sathappan, President, K.Rayavaram Panchayat*

In K.Rayavaram Gram Panchayat of Pudukkottai District, there are three ponds and four tanks. Of these four tanks, two belong to the Public Works Department and the remaining two are under the control of the Panchayat Union. There were encroachments in all the ponds and tanks. Ms.Rani Sathappan knows well that desilting of all these ponds and tanks will help in improving the waver table of the area of the Panchayat. So she approached the

District Collector for permission. As they were PWD tanks, the District Collector directed her to approach the PWD officials and also he recommended to the PWD officials to do the needful. In spite of the Collector's advise, the PWD officials were reluctant to issue a No Objection Certificate. Yet through prolonged persuasion she got the certificate. She evicted the encroachers, desilted the tanks, strengthened the tank bunds and planted trees on the bunds to strengthen the same. Similarly in the ponds also she took efforts to desilt the beds and strengthen the bunds with the help of the community to harvest rain water, enabling improvement in the water table.

### (3) *Ms. Ponnikailasam, President of Anaikuppam Panchayat, Thiruvarur District*

Agriculture is the major source of livelihood to the people settled on the river side of this Panchayat-Anaikuppam. They also depend on the Cauvery river source with its mini tributaries and its channels. But a major portion of the channels were encroached upon for various purposes like agriculture and mining, resulting in poor inflow of water. So the Panchayat President, Ponni Kailasam, decided to evict all the encroachers and to desilt the channels. So she convened a special Gram Sabha for this purpose. After a great struggle she collected all the details about the areas encroached upon from the records. There was a threat to her life by a gang because of this reason. But she didn't tire. She continued her struggle and evicted the encroachers, desilted the channels, planted palymyrah trees on the banks to strengthen them. As a result there is free flow of river water in the channels and also it enables all the ponds and tanks to be filled with water.

### (4) *Keeranur Gram Panchayat Experience of Management of Common Resources – The Water Bodies – Dindigul District*

The main village Keeranur and other hamlets are located at the foothills of the Malleswarar Hill. There are twenty seven ponds/ tanks under the jurisdiction of the Village Panchayat. As agriculture is the major occupation and the majority of the lands are rainfed, protection and maintenance of all water bodies is very important. Hence the Village Panchayat administration decided to give priority to improving the ponds/tanks, canals and streams so that the ground water level will improve. Nattuthurai, President of the Gram Panchayat, acknowledged the training given by the Rajiv Gandhi Chair for Panchayati Raj Studies, Gandhigram Rural Institute in sensitizing the Panchayat leaders on the significance of scientific management of the village commons. Hence it was decided in the Village Panchayat Council not to spend scheme funds on activities other than the watershed activities. Though the expectation of the villagers was generally like provision of sodium vapour lights, CC road, drainage, etc., the reasons for the priority given to the watershed activities were explained to the villagers in the Gram Sabha meetings. Further, with the financial assistance of World Vision of India five watershed works at a cost of about Rs.13.50 lakhs have been successfully carried out, Nattuthurai reported.

### *(5) Thamaraikulam Village Panchayat, Ramnad District*

Mr.S.Sivalingam, President of Thamaraikulam Panchayat of Ramnad District, stated that tanks and ponds are the essential sources for storage of water and the life line of the people. Hence their maintenance, protection and enrichment will help the people to secure their livelihood. Almost all the twelve tanks have been desilted and deepened. As a result the water level of the sub-soil is maintained. Further all the channels which bring water to these tanks have been cleared and are maintained in such a condition that as and when it rains, even the smallest amount of water will reach the tanks without any wastage.

### *(6) Jamruth Beevi, Devipattinam Panchayat*

Ms. Jamruth Beevi, President of Devipatitnam Panchayat of Ramnad District has done a major work by identifying a very big water reserviour which was in dilapidated condition. She got information about the Poovodai tank from the elders of this Panchayat. She interacted with the elders on the reasons for the water table going down to 90 feet when there was a water conservation structure. Water was available at 5 feet depth. She asked what was the water conservation structure. The elders informed her that the Poovodai was the water structure. In 1955 there was heavy rain and, as a result, the Poovodai developed a breach and subsequently there was no repairing of the reservoir. All the years water came to the reservoir and moved away through this breach to the sea.

She started thinking about the Poovodai. When she visited the Poovodai tank she found a lot of encroachments. The coverage of the area is seven km in length and 100 meters in breadth. When the Minister visited her Panchayat, she made a presentation about the condition of the Poovodai and sought assistance. But the Minister, instead of responding to her request, cracked a joke and left the place. The Minister said that the Panchayat has to think of what is possible and feasible. The Poovodai is a troublesome project which cannot be done by the Panchayat. This speech irritated her. She felt very much and made a declaration that the Poovodai will be made a reservoir to save water for the Panchayat. She approached the Collector and explained to him about the Poovodai and got sanction for Rs.25 lakhs under the SGRY scheme. She collected money from the local Jamat and the Saudi Association for this work. They contributed Rs.75,000 for this work. She removed all the encroachments with the help of the people and the district administration. The Poovodai has now been desilted, deepened and seven small tanks have been created. She considers it a major and memorable work done for the community. She commented that it was possible only because of the District Collector who is sincere and sensible on the issues of the rustic folk.

### *(7) Conservation and Management of Water*

Mr.Ponnusamy, President of Semmipalayam Panchayat in Coimbatore District, is not only interested in taking water from the earth and pumping it to the OHT's and from there giving water to individual houses, but also in conserving water through water resource management, natural resource development and conserving soil moisture. According to him people have to be conscientized on rational utilization of water and water conservation for water sustainabaility in the Panchayat area. He got assistance from the MLA and the MP besides the DPAP (Drought Prone Area Programme). He has constructed four check dams at a cost of Rs.5.50 lakhs. He claims that while implementing the check dam project he distributed 3.7 tons of rice to the poor for their work in the project. He generated 528 mandays of employment. Through this work he created an opportunity for 15 wells and 5 borewells to get recharged. All the check dams are very near to the borewells from which water is lifted to the OHTs. Since he got money from the DPAP, it was imperative that watershed committees be formed through which awareness could be created about the importance of water and the severity of drought. Thus people were fully prepared and conscientized on issues of water scarcity and ways and means to avoid it.

Yet another work he carried out was the construction of a rain water harvesting system. In his Panchayat all the 1656 households have created such a structure because of the fact that the people of this village had got the needed orientation already. This work was carried out simultaneously along with the water supply system.

### *(8) Sitharevu Village Panchayat*

Sitharevu is a big Village Panchayat in Athoor Block of Dindigul District with a population of 20,000. There are 16 hamlets in this Village Panchayat. It is a multi-caste and multi-religion Village Panchayat. The Village Panchayat Council has 15 ward members, 10 men and 5 women. Of the total 15 members two are belong to the SC community.

Agriculture and Animal Husbandry are the main source of livelihood of the villagers. Moreover a considerable number of landless agricultural labourers have employment opportunities in plantation estates which are located in the nearby Western Ghats area of Panrimalai.

## Role of Panchayat in Groundwater Management

During the year 2005-06, the DPAP (Drought Prone Area Development Programme) was availed of by the Village Panchayat Council. The farmers met together and identified that the maintenance of three inlet channels was the important work apart from land reclamation and construction of retaining wall to regulate the flood water.

The Village Panchayat took special efforts to mobilize labourers for this work as usually they preferred employment in plantations. Realizing the significance of maintenance work for the inlet channels to ensure the proper flow of rain water into the minor irrigation tanks, the villagers actively participated in the DPAP. At this juncture the NREGA was introduced in this district of Dindigul. Initially the details of the NREGA programmes were not properly explained to the villagers. The President did not give his mind to the implementation of the programme due to his preoccupation with his own affairs. Further it is told that block officials did not give much importance to involving villagers in planning of priorities in the selection of NREGA works. It is learnt that the villagers also did not have much faith in the Village Panchayat administration. Realizing the benefits of the scheme, the local Congress Party leader who had already oriented the Village Panchayat on other public welfare activities, came forward to mobilize the villagers. He, along with a few volunteers and ward members, visited each hamlet and explained the details of the act and the significance of creating/maintaining the Common Property Resources including water bodies in the Village Panchayat.

When the election to the Panchayati Raj Institutions was held in the year 2006, this individual contested in the election and won. After he became the President of Sitharevu Village Panchayat, the NREGA programme implementation was intensified. He showed due respect to the felt needs of the villagers of all hamlets and selected works according to their interest. During the year

2006-07, four projects of desilting and maintenance of minor irrigation tanks have been undertaken. So far 13,000 man days have been generated and about 10 lakh rupees utilized from the allocation of Rs.15.50 lakhs.

The works undertaken under DPAP were maintenance of inlet channels and under NREGA programme the desilting of minor irrigation tanks and small ponds was done. The farmers and common villagers were actively involved in the programme. As they witnessed the filling of tanks during the North-East Monsoon rainfall (July-August), the farmers told that the ground water resource had improved. The President said that it was only because of both maintenance of channels and desilting of tanks and ponds that the ground water sources have been augmented. Earlier, there was no perception amount all stakeholders in this regard. After the emergence of Panchayati Raj Institutions, the villagers have the opportunity to express their felt needs and issues affecting their livelihood which have been properly projected by the Village Panchayat Council. By involving the NREGA the vision of the Village Panchayat and the villagers has been realised.

### *(9) Kameshwaram Panchayat*

Kameshwaram is one of the Village Panchayats in Nagapattinam District, where the NREGP is in progress. In this Panchayat, under the NREGP, the President has given preference to ground water works. There are a number of ponds and tanks in all the hamlets of this Panchayat. The President encouraged and sensitized the people on the need for deepening and proper maintenance of these tanks as it will enable increased ground water which is useful for agricultural activities as well as to the cattle population. He created awareness among the people about the tasks to be performed by them by which it is the responsibility of the people living in the hamlet to maintain them. This made them work with interest in deepening and desilting the tanks located in their hamlets under the NREGP. This new approach of the President has paved the way for improving the water resources in the village.

### *(10) NREG Act – Employment Generation – Poothurai Village Panchayat*

Poothurai is one of the Village Panchayats in Vanur Block of Villupuram District in Tamil Nadu. Poothurai is situated on the border of the Union Territory of Puducherry. It is learnt that Vanur Block is at the tail end of Villupuram District the higher officials' visits are comparatively less than to other blocks of the district. Moreover in Vanur Block there are 65 Village Panchayats and for the sake of administrative convenience it is unofficially—divided into two South Vanur and North Vanur. North Vanur is on the border with Puducherry and Poothurai is the tail end village sharing its jurisdiction with Puducherry. Due to its location, far away from the district headquarters, the frequency of higher officials' visit is less, the villagers said.

Poothurai got its name due to the availability of a variety of flower plants in abundance. There is a lake, named Poothurai Lake and there are ten tanks located in the main village Poothurai and its hamlets, namely, Kondimedu, Kasi Palayam and Manaveli.

### The Village Community

Poothurai is a multi-caste village. The Scheduled Caste (Paraiyar) is the dominant caste. Vanniars are numerically the second dominant group. There are families of Naidu and Pillai castes also. There is communal harmony in Poothurai.

### Village Economy

As there is no system of irrigation facilities, the agricultural activities are mainly rainfed. Now due to failure of monsoon, the farmers prefer casuarina and cashew nut plantations. Paddy cultivation is significantly limited in extent. Due to its proximity to Puducherry, many number of villagers used to go over to Puducherry for employment. Youths, men and women got employment in industrial and other type of agencies functioning in Puducherry.

Animal husbandry is also one of the supplementary income generation activities in Poothurai.

Though there are lakes and tanks in Poothurai, due to lack of interest and community practices in respect of ground water management, the level of the ground water declined. Further due to non-allocation of funds for the protection and promotion of the village commons like forest, water, lake and tanks, the optimum utility of these water bodies is not possible. There is no maintenance work carried out for the past two decades, the villagers told. The implementation of the NREG Act activities since 2006/07 is a boon to the villagers.

## The Role of Village Panchayat in Ground Water Management

When the district officials sensitized the Village Panchayat in respect of the implementation and procedures and priorities under NREGA, the Village Panchayat Council immediately convened the Gram Sabha meeting and discussed with the community. An estimate of Rs.30 lakhs was projected for carrying out NREGA activities like cleaning and maintenance of inlet channels, desilting of Poothurai lake and other 10 water bodies, provision of approach road to burial ground, maintenance work in village roads. After finalizing the project activities under the NREGA Act, the Village Panchayat gave first priority to ground water management. Out of the first instalment of 13 lakh rupees, the Village Panchayat spent Rs.10 lakhs towards activities like maintenance of inlet channel of Poothurai lake. It is a five kilometre distance from the hamlet of Manaveli to Poothurai lake. It has a width of 12 feet to 20 feet. Due to lack of maintenance, in course of time the inlet channel filled up with earth/waste and with growth of wild plants and thorny bushes, its course was disturbed due to encroachment also. Hence in spite of seasonal rains, the water did not reach the lake as it was wasted flowing out at many places.

Now the inlet channel works like removal of thorny bushes, and other wild plants, desilting of beds, strengthening of bunds, and removal of all encroachments are undertaken. The channel is now getting ready to fill the lake. So far about eleven lakh rupees have been spent on this work. The work commenced on 25.11.2006 and about 73 days were spent to complete the work. On an average daily 230 workers, mostly women labourers, are engaged in this work. They have received Rs.80 per day as wages to complete the unit of work assigned by the Village Panchayat. The facilities like provision of protected drinking water to the workers at the site, ensuring arrangement to look after the children of workers, availability of first aid box to attend to any untoward injury and provision of medical care to those who suffered major injury have been properly dealt with by the Panchayat administration.

The work is really an endurable one and very much useful to the villagers, the vice-President claimed. He said that more than a decade ago, the Government had done the maintenance work in the inlet channel. But the work was not properly carried out due to non involvement of the people. The work under the NREGA is perfectly done. In spite of handships, the workers gave their energy and mind to the successful implementation, the vice-President added.

The Panchayat clerk said that there is a lack of time to do the procedural activities like maintenance of muster roll, obtaining signature for attendance, entry in the job card, distribution of wage amount and obtaining the signature for the receipt of wage amount etc. in addition to the allocation of work at the work site as well as monitoring of the execution of works. At a time an average of 200 to 250 workers turned up for the work. Effective monitoring is a challenge, the Makkal Nala Paniyalar who is also entrusted with the responsibility of implementation of NREG Act activities. The staff shared that many women in the disguise of attending to work nature used to while away time; elderly women are not able to contribute to complete the task. They felt that the villagers have not yet realized the significance of the scheme. The villagers have the opinion that since it is the government's money, why should the Panchayat insist on measurement? The Panchayat staff demanded that there should be a systematic implementation phase wise, area-wise and real felt need-wise. The salary of the Makkal Nala Paniyalar lower than the worker's and in that case how could be monitor the work of the workers, the clerk shared. Moreover the clerk observed that the spirit and interest among the villagers was seen earlier is diminishing now as the Government Officials do not emphasize on the measurement.

The Poothurai Panchayat President is a woman. Though she is educated she does not have orientation in public activities. She conducts Panchayat Council meetings and organize Gram Sabha meetings only. The rest of the activities are looked after by her son, who is in politics. The workers shared that the NREG Act is a good relief to them as in the agricultural operations the wage is low and also there is no scope for sustainable employment to all. They demanded that the activities under the NREG Act should be planned and implemented every year and employment should be given to at least one member in each family in the rural area, they added.

### *(11) Vanagiri Village Panchayat*

Vanagiri Village Panchayat is in Sirkali Block of Nagapattinam District. It is a multi-caste village located in the coastal area. Patinavar (Fishermen Community) is the majority community. Padaiyachi (Vanniyar), Naidu and SC are the other main communities of the Village Panchayat, Vanagiri. There are six hamlets, namely, Keela Vanagiri, Mela Vanagiri, Naganathamkoi, Palayagaram, Eramapalayam and Dosaikulam. It is a big village having a population of about eight thousand citizens. Agriculture and fishing are the main occupations in Vanagiri Panchayat. In the year 2006 when the NREGA was introduced in the state of Tamil Nadu, in the District of Nagapattinam, Vanagiri Village Panchayat was the first Village Panchayat where the NREGA programme was commenced on 02.03.2006.

The Gram Sabha meeting was convened to select and prioritize the works under NREGA and the villagers listed desilting of tanks, maintenance of channels and road work in their hamlets. Moreover as the villagers suffered due to entry of sea-water during the recent tsunami disaster, there was a suggestion to construct a protective bund along the coastal area so that the salination of agricultural land due to entry of sea-water could be prevented. As the majority of the villagers preferred the construction of the protection bund, the proprietor of one the shrimp farm which is established along the wasted area came forward to spare a 30 meter length of his own land so that the construction would be purposeful.

The protection bund was constructed at an average height of about 2½ meter which will not only prevent the entry of sea-water but also protect ground-water and agricultural land from salinity. Daily about 350 workers, mostly women, are involved in the work. The turnout of workers was very low during the first week of the implementation. Later, understanding the individual as well as the community benefits, the community extended its cooperation and the workers turned out in large numbers and in the year 2006-2007 other activities like maintenance of drainage channel and inlet channel and three minor irrigation tanks have been undertaken. So far (upto July 2007) Rs.11.00 lakhs has been utilised for the implementation of these activities, the Panchayat clerk explained.

The President shared that though desilting of tanks and maintenance of channels were the works demanded by one section of the community, the serious threats of salination of ground-water, entry of sea water into the farm area and the pollution of soil were realized and the construction of a protection bund was preferred by the majority. After the completion of this work, the desilting and maintenance of water bodies have been undertaken, he added. The researcher found the sensitization among the community members in respect of ground water management has been steadily enhanced after the tsunami. And when the Village Panchayat was entrusted with the responsibility of NREGA implementation, they rationally acted to protect and promote ground water conservation.

In the context of failure of the State institutions in managing the commons and natural resources Governments seek an alternative. It is natural that they have to dig into the past and trace it from history. Communities are effective managers and they manage the natural resources by following community laws. The community once had experts for this purpose. Till the introduction of the 73rd Amendment to the Constitution of India some of the commons were managed by the Government and some were abandoned. The New Panchayati Raj System has created space for such activities within the domain of the Panchayat. The Panchayat Act provides only guidelines. The leaders who have got commitment and sensitivity have done commendable work. Lot of innovations are being done by the women leaders. It raises the hope that Panchayati Raj Institutions can do this kind of activities.

## REFERENCES

G.Palanithurai, *Leadership Matters in Grassroots Governance*, Pathfinders Series-4 (Mono), Gandhigram: Rajiv Gandhi Chair for Panchayati Raj Studies, 2006.

G.Palanithurai, *Leadership Matters in Grassroots Governance*, Pathfinders Series-18 (Mono), Gandhigram: Rajiv Gandhi Chair for Panchayati Raj Studies, 2006.

G.Palanithurai, *Leadership Matters in Grassroots Governance*, Pathfinders Series-14 (Mono), Gandhigram: Rajiv Gandhi Chair for Panchayati Raj Studies, 2006.

G.Palanithurai, *Leadership Matters in Grassroots Governance*, Pathfinders Series-19 (Mono), Gandhigram: Rajiv Gandhi Chair for Panchayati Raj Studies, 2006.

G.Palanithurai, *Leadership Matters in Grassroots Governance*, Pathfinders Series-1 (Mono), Gandhigram: Rajiv Gandhi Chair for Panchayati Raj Studies, 2006.

G.Palanithurai, *Leadership Matters in Grassroots Governance*, Pathfinders Series-2 (Mono), Gandhigram: Rajiv Gandhi Chair for Panchayati Raj Studies, 2006.

G.Palanithurai, *Tamil Nadu Panchayati Raj System*, New Delhi: Concept Publishing Company, 2004.

Madhav Gadgil, "Grassroots Conservation Practices: Revitalising the Traditions", Ashish Kothari et.al (eds), *Communities and Conservation*, New Delhi: Sage Publications, 1998.

N.S.Jodha, *Life on the Edge*, New Delhi:, Oxford University Press, 2001.

S.N.Bhise (ed), *Decolonizing the Commons*, New Delhi: National Foundation for India, 2004.

V.Ragupathy, *Participatory Management of Natural Resources: Irrigation Tanks in Panchayats*, New Delhi: Concept Publishing Company, 2004.

# 5

# Local Communities and Water Management Issues

*G. Palanithurai*

## Introduction

Water and issues related to water remain on the top of development discourse all over the world. Water opens up avenues for dispute as much as the possibility for cooperation between and amongst communities. Perception about water keeps changing not only geographically and temporally but also based on the use and the user. Similarly, perspectives keep expanding and issues relating to water is getting revised based on the context and the vitality of the use to which water is put to by a given community. Especially, in an agrarian economy where water is a vital livelihood resource, the significance attached to water is omnipotent and supreme.

The problem human race faces with water is that either it is unmanageably abundant or critically scarce. However, the condition of water being plentiful is hardly for a few weeks in a year. Otherwise, it is 'water crisis' that India spells for rest of the whole year. As far as production, distribution and management of water services are concerned, in India water used to be provided by the public sector, since it is usually considered as a typical public good. The power of globalization processes and the framework of sector reform measures of the Government over the years have silently brought about radical changes in the management and distribution of water resources and services in India.

For instance, according to market sources in India, the packaged water industry is estimated to be more than Rs.10,000 crore and is growing at a rapid pace of about 30 – 35 per cent. With growing ground-water pollution, large number of people particularly in the urban centres are hooked to packaged drinking water. Although it accounts for about 6 per cent of the total beverage market in India, branded bottled water is the fastest growing industry in the beverage sector. It is estimated that the single largest share in the mineral water market might still belongs to Parle's Bisleri brand, which has about 35 per cent market penetration. Multinationals such as Pepsi and Coke have been extremely successful in edging out many smaller brands. Behind this silver lining, many environmentalists have attributed depletion of ground-water in various parts of the country to over extraction of water by packaged or bottled water industry.

## Controversial Concepts

In Tamil Nadu for about a decade now, issues relating to water rights, commodification of water, privatization of water resources, privatization of water distribution services, and commercial draft of water and so on which were being sporadically discussed and that which remained as agenda for discussion at policy-making forums, have become vital issues for discussion including at the Panchayat level. The mindset of taking water as a tradable commodity in the market place has erupted several controversies in the power related domains of the State and the local community.

Some argue that this market-oriented culture is a mindset brought about by globalization processes. Trading is gaining prime place even in natural resources, such as water and river sand, beyond the normal replenishing capacity of the nature. Challenges of this sort have become common-place to the traditional water rights and means of livelihoods of the rural community. The Rajiv Gandhi Chair for Panchayati Raj Studies of Gandhigram Rural Institute with the assistance of the Ford Foundation has been able to capture the root cause and the ramifications of the spread of water markets in Tamil Nadu. This paper briefly brings out the instances and the ramifications of globalization with specific reference to water.

A series of questions have cropped up in the context of privatization of water resources and liberalization of investments in the sphere of trading water as a commodity. They include: Who does the water resources belong to? That is, water being one of the vital livelihood resources, is it a common property resource, which the local community has granted the trusteeship to the State to regulate and safeguard? or is it a property of the State that it (the State) can decide in whatever way it deems fit to run the Government? What is the space for local bodies in approving and or regulating the use of water resources by local people for various purposes? What is expected to be the reaction of the local bodies when the State decides to allocate for free (or sell for a price) water resources of one village to a neighbouring village that is starving for water? So much so, what is supposed to be the reaction of local bodies when the State decides to put on sale water resources to an MNC as a gesture of promoting FDI in the State? These are some of the key research questions that this empirical enquiry tried to find answers for.

The contexts of these empirical studies have been places where with the approval of the State government - ignoring the livelihood questions and usufractory sentiments of the local government – several MNCs are progressively taking control of water resources and water services in Tamil Nadu. They have made 'water markets' and have spread a culture of defining water as a 'commodity'. The concern has been in defining the role of local bodies and other local institutions in taking up these challenges and nurturing both formal and informal governance mechanisms in handling these situations.

Excerpts have been drawn from four case studies. They are : (1) the controversy over Coca Cola trying to set up a water bottling company at the SIPCOT premises in Gangaikondan, Thirunelveli; (2) provision of water to 11 Village Panchayats through Public Private Partnership arrangement in Thirupur; (3) commercial draft of water in various places in Tamil Nadu and the community unrest about it; (4) the Sector Reform Project of the Government of India that experiments with Village Panchayats to take up water distribution services.

## Case-1 : Gangaikondan - Globalization in its Logical Minimum

'Gangaikondan' in Tirunelveli is on the news for quite sometime now. On the surface, it is a dispute over extraction of Thamiraparani water for manufacturing aerated drink by South India Bottling Company, established by the Coca Cola. Going by the nature of issues the dispute brings forth, one can say that it is globalization in microcosm at the community level. Since July 2005 when this problem started emerging, it has taken various shapes and several turns. Local NGOs and the Communist Parties of India have played key role in putting across to the community the repercussions of Coke's proposal.

One of the vital events is that the community leaders from Gangaikondan, in batches, have visited Plachimada in Kerala to see for themselves the havoc Coke has played with the ground water aquifers and to the livelihoods of the people who live in about 10 km radius from Plachimada. The lesson they brought from Kerala about Coca Cola was: "*It is destroying livelihoods, stealing water and poisoning land. This is the story of Coca Cola in Kerala*". Every time a batch returned from Plachimada the community disapproval and protest against commencing the Coke Unit at the SIPCOT premises in Gangaikondan seemed to have been getting stronger and powerfully built.

As per the Panchayats Act, the South India Bottling Company needs to obtain No Objection Certificate (NOC) from the Village Panchayat. Mr Kamsan, President of Gangaikondan Village Panchayat initially opposed the idea—then supported it—then died of jaundice, it is reported. Rumors have it that the President drinks like a fish and so the Company people gave him a lethal cocktail of drinks and bought him for a price. The Vice-President Mr Perumal has been allowed to serve as acting President now. The company is yet to get the No Objection Certificate (NOC) from the Panchayat.

The new President is one among those who visited Plachimada. Some local NGOs and a few CPI activists [including an Ex-MLA of the CPI (M)] seem to be behind him and with the protesters. The new President is opposing the Coke and is an active member of the Thamiraparani Protection Committee, promoted by local NGOs. The irony is there is also a section of the local people who support that the Coke must start functioning in Gangaikondan. These supporters led by an Ex-MLA of the DMK Party have formed SIPCOT Entrepreneurs Protection Committee. The Coke Company is said to be behind in setting the agenda of this Committee. So, Gangaikondan stood divided.

The views of the SIPCOT Entrepreneurs Protection Committee are that: (i) the Company has assured employment to at least ten people from each one of the 12 habitations of Gangaikondan; (ii) the Company has been allowed to take 900,000 liters of water per day from the flowing Thamiraparani river and not through drilling boreholes; and (iii) preventing Coke from commencing production might scare away other investors coming to the SIPCOT at Gangaikondan.

The stand of protestors are that: (i) the employment attraction the Company shows is a myth and that they would provide employment to manual labourers for a short period of two-three years; (ii) 900,000 liters per day could be on paper and that there is no mechanism to watch if they draw only 900,000 liters a day and that if they have not drilled additional boreholes in side the 32 acres of land they have acquired from SIPCOT area, where no body, including Vandana Siva, is permitted to enter; (iii) more than the water they draw it is the effluent that has damaged the lands and livelihoods in Plachimada and what is the assurance that it would not recur in Gangaikondan; (iv) and finally, *can't human species live without coke?*

There are a few more points to touch upon so as to make it complete within the brevity aimed at here. First, if SIPCOT should provide water to an industry whose 95 per cent of the input is water? Secondly, the very fact that the Company is enticing with money almost everyone even at the village level stands as a proof of the amount of money they expect in return; Thirdly, given the few industries that have been started now in the SIPCOT premises, if one company is assured of 900,000 litres of water from where would other hundreds of industries, to be set up, get water for their use? Some of the community members suspect that the company might do some palm greasing and go in for ground water extraction. Fourthly, the issue of communalism in Gangaikondan area which got subsided over a decade ago is being renewed, so that the community would be busy fighting for nothing, while Coke does business peacefully. Finally and very importantly, the Local Bodies being told by the Bureaucracy to cancel the Gram Sabha meeting on the pretext that a Gram Sabha meeting might end up as a communal conflict. The 2nd October 2005 Gram Sabha meeting was postponed to 20th November 2005 and again it has been postponed indefinitely. Will the 26th January 2006 Gram Sabha meeting be held remains an unanswered question.

## Case - 2 : Privatization of Water Services

As part of sector reform measures, the Government of Tamil Nadu for the first time has gone in for Public Private Partnership (PPP) in providing water for the industries in Tirupur town and for a few villages in Tirupur Block. This is called BOOT (Build-Own-Operate-Transfer) model water supply scheme. The estimated cost of the project is Rs.1,023 crores which includes water supply and sewage systems. Mahindra & Mahindra, Bechtel and the United Utilities of UK are the main contractors besides Hindustan Construction Corporation and Larsen & Tourbo. It is called 'Mahindra Consortium' for short. The Consortium has registered a company called New Tirupur Area Development Corporation Limited (NTADCL), specially for the purpose of this project. It is a 30-year contract arrangement at the end of the 30th year it would be handed over to the Government.

Users should pay for water on the basis of the quantity used is one significant move the NTADCL has made. This Project has become operational now. Water supplied to industries are charged

Rs.45 per 1000 litres (in addition Rs.25,000 deposit demanded). Water supplied to the Village Panchayats should be paid at Rs.3.50 per 1000 litres. Village Panchayats (VPs) receive water bills from NTADCL direct.

This project is expected to benefit (i) the industries, (ii) the slum dwellers, and (iii) the way-side villages in the same order as mentioned. The analysis of some of the VP functionaries is that it is primarily for the industries in Tirupur, secondarily for the slum dwellers most of whom are workers in those industries, and the remaining water is distributed to the way-side VPs. The reasons for the variation in the degree of importance are obvious. The industries should survive. The workers in the industries, most of them migrants from poorer rural areas of Tamil Nadu, should be received of the water crunch so that they work for the industries. Thirdly, the way-side VPs the water passes through, if by-passed, would become a persistent headache to the TWAD Board and to Tirupur Municipality by agitations and protests.

The question of some of the VP functionaries in Tirupur is that, going by water policy and developmental ethics, water for drinking purposes should get the top most priority. But, industries have got overriding priority in the NTADCL agreement. Clearly, water as a commercial venture (as one of the factors of production with certain money value) is more likely to succeed in Industries rather than giving it to the villages for drinking purposes. This proves that the basic tenet of NTADCL like any other private business venture is commercial viability or RoI (Return on Investment) which the Government of Tamil Nadu has paid heed to. They have also made a provision that if any VPs demand more water they can buy it from the company at the rates it is given to the industries. This raises the issue of rich-poor divide where equity in distribution is at stake.

The VP functionaries show a calculation that indicates that if the NTADCL agreed to supply (of course, on payment of Rs.3.50 per 1000 lr.) all the water a Village Panchayat requires the VP can save a lot of money they spend on EB bill (water pumping charges) and the regular pump maintenance expenses. One of the serious problems of most Panchayats, that is 'fat EB bill', can be brought down spectacularly. But, the quantity supplied, as of now, is not even one fourth of what is required at the Panchayat level. One of the reasons for this is that the NTADCL goes by 1991 census in the year 2006. The VPs are told to take it for granted because Bhavani water (the source of water for NTADCL) is meant primarily for the industries.

One postulate of this research was that the Village Panchayats would be discontented that water services have been privatized. Response in most villages[1] disproved it and that the Village Panchayats do not mind receiving water from private water service providers. In fact, this arrangement can reduce VP level expenses on water supply, as shown through calculations by some VP functionaries. But they want the NTADCL to commit to provide the quantum demanded by the VPs. If this is not done, they would end up paying additionally to NTADCL. Apart from the questions of quantity, affordability and transparency, one apprehension that most VPs raise is of 'accountability'. There is no grievance redressal mechanism to the users. When a grievance is taken to the notice of NTADCL, 'there are only cross-references given and no answers to have the grievance redressed'.

## Case - 3 : Commercial Draft of Water

There was a time in the recently liberalized past when people didn't quite know how to refer to a new product called 'drinking water'. They would say 'bottled water' and 'mineral water' to freely refer to one or the other kind of water, perhaps meaning the same one. It used to be confusing. People were not used to drinking that had had to be bought. People were getting used to paying money to drink water. 2002 should be called the year of packaged water. As a December 2002 newspaper article headline puts it, "water Biz on a Boil". The article expands on this suggestive phrase: "The Rs.1000 crore packaged water segment outperformed beverage categories such as carbonated soft drinks, tea and coffee, and powder drinks".

Branded bottled water is the fastest growing industry in the beverage sector. Market growth rate has been an unimaginable 80 per cent plus at the beginning of the year 2000. Competition is hot; 2002 witnessed large scale consolidation, with smaller players being gradually edging out by the big contenders.

According to BIS, there are 1,200 bottled water factories all over India, of which (600 are in Tamil Nadu). It is estimated to be growing at a rate of 40-50 per cent annually over the past four years (2004). In Chennai alone, more than 200 legal and 400 illegal bottled water manufacturers operate. India's packaged water industry is barely a decade old and it is earning in billions. Brand names such as Coke's Kinley, Pepsi's Aquafina and the Indian bottled water giant Parle's Bisleri enjoy a Rs. 4 billion market, according to reports.

Coca Cola, for instance, sources a bulk of its kinley brand of bottled water with a factory in Athoor Village in Chozhavaram Block of Thiruvallur district about 40 km from Chennai. Besides this, there are several other local brands of water, most of them run by business people from Chennai and Kancheepuram. The attraction being: the water is sweet and rich in mineral contents. Generally soil in Athoor is sandy which has the capacity of holding water for long. Athoor is located close to *Kusasthalaaru* (a branch of *Cholavaramyeri*) plus the popular *Puzhalyeri* is situated about 5 kilometres from Athoor. These considerations can set the mind at rest that investment in water business would be worth it.

The story goes like this... Athoor Village Panchayat granted approval (NOC) in the year 1998 to a request made by a rich local farmer to sell water drawn from the water sources at his land. He has started bottling fresh water in the name of 'Hallo'. In the year 2002 the coca-cola entered into an agreement with 'Hallo', increased production capacity, expanded the market and started selling water bottles in the name of 'Kinley'. An application to draw extra water and to sell it in the name of MVR Mineral water was turned down by the Village Panchayat on the grounds that it might affect agriculture and drinking water supply. Now the factory runs three units in Athoor. There are about 20 vehicles of kinley carrying water as much as 3.5 lakh litres of water daily.

Again in 2002 a new mineral water company was set up in Athoor in the name of 'Plus'. After objection by Village Panchayat it had to relocate to Nagalapuram in Andhra Pradesh. Similarly, a water company (known as *Achi moru*) disguised as producing and selling *moru* (butter milk pockets) and Rasna pockets started drawing water also for sale. The villagers objected and the company had to leave the village. One of the major demands for water comes from the Chennai Metro. The water requirements of the Lorries that have entered into contract with Chennai Metro used to take water in large quantities. Despite explanation that it is taken by Chennai Metro Water as an obligation to provide water to the citizenry in Chennai Corporation, the Village Panchayat stopped it. After a few days local farmers started selling water to the Metro Water Lorries, not in huge quantities though. This practice continues even now.

Several business people are reported to have tried to set up water plants in Athoor (e.g. Kokulam Water). But they have been wound up by the villagers through protests. As of now, one water company (with three plants) that operates in Athoor is Kinley with the support of the local Halo. The owner of 'Halo' is said to be a local big farmer. Moreover there are about 75 families from Athoor alone who work as labourers in this Kinley water plants. Hence, the villagers are not in a position to force Kinley to quit.

One supposition, which has been proved right in several similar studies, is that overdraft of groundwater leads to depletion affecting agricultural pursuits. To put it a little more clearly, when there is competing demand between 'water for agricultural operations' and 'water for commercial bottling units', the former, most probably, would get sidelined, unless there is severe opposition and protests from the local community against commercial draft of water. This fact is confirmed from Athoor also. If we can stretch this to a stage of imaginary future, where the community completely stands deprived of water, it would lead to a situation for the community putting an end to the market by violent protest, which can be called limit to the market. The following is a rapid assessment of how the commercial draft of water in Athoor has affected the local community.

## Pursuits in Agriculture

### *Livelihoods Lost*

As per the records of the Village Administrative Officer, cultivable lands in Athoor are owned by about 200 farmers. About 15 of them are big farmers and 185 of them are small and marginal farmers. The mineral water companies and tankers of Chennai Metro Water are continuously drawing water using hi-power submersible pumps. The water level that used to be at 20– 22 feet has gone down to 120–180 feet. Besides increasing in-put prices and escalating pumping charges, the depleting water table has made agriculture unattractive and non-remunerative in Athoor area. Many of the small and marginal farmers are selling out their lands to business people (*Saettu*) from Chennai, who buy it for making house plots. Those who still keep their lands have converted their lands – either in full or in part – as brick kilns to supply to the construction works that is booming in the city.

### *Alternative Livelihoods*

There are about 560 agricultural wage earners in Athoor. The agricultural wage earners have also found employment in agriculture non-dependable and the wages to be too meagre. They commute by Lorries and tankers to Chennai to earn better wages in construction works with building contractors in Chennai. Some of them who are not very much mobile have become menial workers in local brick kilns. There are others (about 75 families) who are employed in local water bottling companies. Another peril that is taking place is sand mining in *Kusasthala aru* which is also a reason for water depletion. There are some local people of Athoor involved in sand mining for a wage.

## *Drinking Water*

The village has three ponds and 7 Panchayat borewells. They run dry during summer. Availability of even drinking water becomes difficult during summer seasons. Then, the residents start reprimanding the water companies. Once, it rains and water availability becomes normal, they forget all about the water scarcity and about the water companies return to normalcy. The companies go on. The Pollution Control Board that tested the water for its mineral content has reported that the mineral content in the water has come down from 75 per cent to 25 per cent in the past few years. They have also warned them of water turning saline if water draft continued at the rate it is done now.

## *No Water Companies any More*

Private people even now approach Athoor Panchayat seeking permission to draw water for commercial purposes. The Village Panchayat in its meeting held on 30th December 2005 has passed a resolution that no water company would be allowed to set up their unit at Athoor. Some people raised voice that a resolution should be passed to evict the Kinley bottling company also from Athoor. Considering the number of families (75 families) that earn their wage from the bottling company, and not being able to suggest an alternative employment to them, resolution to that effect was not passed.

Halo minerals, the contract bottler for Coke's Kinley brand of water, is accused of depleting the groundwater in Athoor village. Disturbingly, Kinley's bottling units are located in an area that has been declared 'critical' because of the plentiful sweet water available underground and because of the areas importance to the water security of the region and the city of Chennai.

An overview of Chozhavaram Block gives a gloomy picture again. Many of the Panchayats in Chozhavaram Block has at least one mineral water bottling company. In some villages though not a company, there is water tanker operation taking place. Hardly any of them bother to get Panchayat permission. Agricultural operations have shrunk in Village Panchayats such as Athoor, Alinjampakkam and Alamathy mainly due to commercial draft of water coupled with urbanization. The *Chozhavaram yeri* being mostly used for taking water for Chennai population by the Chennai Metro Water tankers is also a reason for the crisis.

The Villages where commercial draft began in 1998 are found to be more seriously defaced, compared to the ones where water companies have started operating recently, about 2–3 years ago. The recent rains (November 2005) have, to a considerable extent, reduced the cry of the people for water. Otherwise there is a vast shift in livelihood patterns seen in many of the villages (Erumaipattypalayam, Karanodai, Alinjampakkam, Chozhavaram and Alamathi): people shifting from agriculture to construction and other works in the cities. Their water has been stolen and it has made them sell out their lands, and finally it is sad to notice some people earning their wages as menial worker in the water bottling companies.

## The Changing Paradigms

There are two paradigms of water in intense contest - the paradigm of water as commons and the paradigm of water as a commodity. Water is common because its equitable allocation and sustainability depend on the cooperation between members of a community[1]. Access to water as a commonly shared public good prevails even today in most places of the country, whereas on the other side privatization of water resources is also gaining momentum with profit-orientation and economic thinking that globalization trains people in Athoor (and Mathur, another village severely affected near here) in Tamil Nadu are real-life examples to prove this point.

Gone are the days when the extent of land one holds and the amount of crop one harvests determined the social status of a person in Tamil Nadu society. The market and commodity orientation has redefined that 'cash in hand or cash at bank' as the prime determinants of status in the society. This is evident from the fact that they quit agriculture and turn to selling water at Mathur and in the villages at the vicinity.

The profitability of this business is beyond question. Coke's Indian operations took a beating in the first few years of operation after fizzy drinks failed to perform to company expectations. But after Kinley, Coke's water brand, was launched in mid-2000, the multinationals revenues nosed up. In fact, Coca Cola India's third quarter 2001 results mention that "its growth of 11 per cent had been led by the successful expansion of Kinley water." For companies it is profit and to the communities it is loss of a vital livelihood resource.

Despite Groundwater (Regulation) Act the Government is not in a position to curb the menace of groundwater extraction. This is because during summer seasons unless people turn to private water suppliers the Government machinery in charge of providing water would be in great trouble not being able to supply water. Failure to provide water for drinking for quite a few months might tell not only upon the performance of a given Government but also upon the life of the Government itself.

### Case – 4 : Community Management of Rural Water Supply Service

Rajiv Gandhi Drinking Water Mission of the Government of India has experimented a decentralized model in managing rural water supply. This came about after the introduction of New Panchayati Raj System in India. Decentralization policies contribute to reducing over-concentration of power, authority, and resources at the level of Central or the Provincial Government. The aim is achieving a greater equity in the allocation of resources, with increased efficiency, effectiveness and sustainability of water services. The major consequence of decentralisation is that it increased the financial, operational, technical and managerial responsibilities at the local level. It has also happened sometimes with some Panchayats not having the capacity to meet such a challenge, training and capacity-building programmes have been undertaken by TWAD Board of the Government of Tamil Nadu, foreign donor agencies such as the Danida, and the Rajiv Gandhi Chair at Gandhigram Rural Institute.

The research team working on Global and Local Newsletter at GRI could find in several villages where drinking water sector reform projects were implemented that there is a management system getting established, not as a parallel to the Panchayati Raj System but as an extension of it. It sends across good news that water as a vital livelihood asset can be managed at the Panchayat level.

India is fortunate to have the Panchayati Raj Institutions (PRI) System. It provides a sound logical basis for democracy, development and administration. In the Sector Reform Project implemented by Government of Tamil Nadu the institutional foundation lies within the framework of PRI. The Village Panchayat has the formal responsibility to operate domestic water supply (Panchayat Act, 1994). The core institution is the Village Water and Sanitation Committee (VWSC) of the VP (Panchayat Rules, 1999) and VWSC consists of leaders selected by the Gram Sabha. VWSC represents the community and the legal basis within PRI is clear.

The Government of Tamil Nadu has issued a Government Order (No. 260, 1998) regarding collection of and payment for house service connection. It provides the necessary legal basis for revenue collection. Efforts are made by some Projects with sector reform agenda such as Rajiv Gandhi Drinking Water Mission Project, *Swajaldhara* Project, Danida WS Project to operationalise this concept. Wherever attempts were made to make sincere use of PRIs, success could be seen. The lesson is that building a management structure that can achieve technically and financially sustainable water supplies are needed before investing in more new facilities that will be poorly maintained and not deliver demanded services. *Wherever attempts are made to make sincere use of PRIs, success could be seen in establishing a sound management system at the local level.*

## Decentralization Works

Influence of decentralization concept in the sector reform measures of the Government has given the responsibility of operating and maintaining rural water supply out to the Village Panchayats. These have been carried out especially on experimental basis by agencies of the Government such as Rajiv Gandhi Drinking Water Mission or through bi-lateral arrangement by agencies such as the Danida with Government of Tamil Nadu. Apart from these, there are also Village Panchayats that have experimented Panchayat-based management of water supply system by self-initiative. Examples can be cited of: Keerapalayam in Cuddalore district, Michalepattinam in Ramanathapuram district, Semmipalayam in Coimbatore district, and Veerapandianpattinam near Kayalpatinam.

### *Keerapalayam*

This Village Panchayat with a population of 5350 is a Model Village Panchayat on several counts such as water, sanitation, environmental cleanliness, freedom from alcohol, and rainwater harvesting. Dr A P J Abdul Kalam visited this village a year ago and congratulated the Village Panchayat President and the other Panchayat functionaries. All the 1160 households have individual household toilets. There is a Village Water and Sanitation Committee which takes care of the operation and maintenance relating to water supply. All House Service Connection holders pay water charges at the rate of Rs.30 a month, and the users of common water collection points pay at the rate of Rs.5 a month. This contributes to paying the pumping charges and maintenance of water supply installations, which ensures uninterrupted water supply. There are handpumps provided in almost all the streets which cater to the drinking water needs during power failure. A Danida project that was implemented in Cuddalore district has also substantially assisted them to establish this management system in Keerapalayam.

### *Veerapandianpattinam*

This Panchayat is an excellent example for how a Village that was water starved could get adequate and uninterrupted drinking water supply because of the efforts of the Village Panchayat and the understanding of the community members. When Panchayat President assumed office, the immediate problem he had to set right was the problem of irregular water supply. He found that the Village Panchayat gets water from a combined water supply scheme, and the Panchayat did not pay the Electricity Bill due to the TWAD Board for several months. The Panchayat Office stroke a bargain with the TWAD Board, whereby the TWAD agreed to provide uninterrupted water supply provided the Panchayat pays a caution deposit of six months Electricity bill. It worked out to Rs.88,000.

The Panchayat convened a Gram Sabha Meeting and explained the position, where a few meaningful resolutions were passed such as: (1) hike the House Tax and Generate income, and (2) all the House Service Connection holders to pay monthly water charges at the Panchayat Office regularly. The Panchayat regularly pays the Electricity bill and there is uninterrupted water supply in the Village. Later locally five OHTs have been constructed and the cell phone numbers of tank operators are with the community to make complaints, if any. Now, the system has grown to the extent of people paying penalty for delayed water charges payment. This has become another model that manages water supply.

### *Semmipalayam*

Generally, Tamil Nadu villages have a Dalit colony that is a little away from the main settlement. Usually all the common facilities and community infrastructure are located in the main settlement where the cast Hindu live. As per Government records those facilities are for sharing by the Dalits as well. But in most villages this sharing (especially sharing of water) with Dalits is a source of problem. Semmipalayam is no exception to this. The Dalit colony was not getting adequate water supply, and those who approach the main settlement for taking water used to be insulted by the caste Hindus. The then newly elected Panchayat President thought something had to be done about it.

He made an application to the TWAD Board to get the financial assistance of Rajiv Gandhigram Drinking Water Mission's Sector Reform Project to construct additional Over Head Tanks in the Dalits Colonys. The Project demanded 10 per cent community contribution and an undertaking that operation and maintenance would be taken care of by the Village Panchayat. Six OHTs were constructed at a cost of Rs.45 lakhs for which the community contributed Rs.4.5 lakhs. Each household had to pay Rs.3,200. The scheme got completed. All the households at the Dalit Colony got house service connection; all the local schools and common buildings also receive adequate water. There are no common water collection points. Even washing platforms have been provided. All the residents pay water charges regularly and are paying the Electricity bill. Water that was a source of conflict in Semmipalayam is no more so. The able leadership of the Village Panchayat leader deserves admiration.

### *Michalepattinam*

This is a Model Panchayat for local initiative on constructing Rain Water Harvesting structures (RWH). Ms. Jesumary, the Panchayat President of Michalepattinam is one of those few who have clearly understood what is meant by saying: 'water is the source of life'. She found that water for drinking and water for agricultural purposes are in acute scarcity especially because people do not bother to, or do not know how to harvest water when it is plenty and how to store it under the ground. She explained in one of the Gram Sabha meetings that RWH at every household would solve many of the problems associated with water scarcity including drinking water and water for irrigation. She convened the Panchayat meeting again to discuss among the members how to install this structure and how to enable people to do this. The Panchayat resolved to help each and every house to install a pucca rainwater harvesting structure. The Panchayat provided sand and stones to each house. The Panchayat purchased PVC pipes for the entire village and distributed to them to ensure quality of the RWH structure.

The Panchayat consulted specialists in RWH and created an innovative technique of connecting all the rain outlet pipes from all the households to a common pipe to harvest the rainwater. This rainwater harvesting structure has been put up in such a way that the entire rainwater would be stored without wasting a drop from each roof. Rainwater from the roof of the houses run through a PVC pipe and all such PVC pipes from all the houses on both the sides of the streets are connected to a larger PVC pipe which has been laid down in the middle of the street, which takes the water to a tank. Whereas in many of the households in Tamil Nadu RWH structures constructed as a state-driven requirement, in Michalepattinam, Ms. Jesumary has made it fruitful to the entire community.

## Analysis

As part of overall sector reform measures, and taking cue from the suggestion given by the World Bank - the largest donor to India in the area of water - the Government of India has put down in the 'National Water Policy 2002' that "*Private sector participation should be encouraged in ... water resources projects....... Depending upon the specific situations, various combinations of private sector participation, in building, owning, operating, leasing and transferring water resources facilities may be considered*".

This Policy revision of the GoI backed by the liberalized Foreign Direct Investment (FDI) has led to proliferation of several modes of water privatization, where water production and distribution are partially or fully assigned to private operators through franchise bidding process. They are variously called such as: (a) Service Contracts, (b) BOOT (Build, Operate, Own and Transfer), and (c) Divestiture (transferring the full ownership and responsibility of the water system including the water source to a private operator etc.). They estimate that the market for bottled drinking water alone in India is Euro 200 million, with a potential of reaching Euro 10 to 15 billion. MNC majors like Coca Cola, Pepsi, and Nestle, are already significant players in the market besides a large number of Indian brands. Thus, private corporations are progressively taking control of water resources and water services in several States including Tamil Nadu (e.g., Thirupur). They have made 'water markets' and are fast spreading a culture of defining water as a 'commodity'.

These developments have made two things refutable. First, the aspect of equity and social justice in water distribution meaning 'can poor people buy water for a price at the rates dictated by the private operators' and secondly, an important milestone that addresses issues of constitutional authority and jurisdiction is the 74th Constitutional Amendment, which recognizes State Level Local Bodies, and empowers them to plan and administer water supply projects within their jurisdiction including rights to create tariff structures. This has been refuted as well. So much so, the National Water Policy 2002 again notes that Water Users Associations and the local bodies such as Municipalities and Gram Panchayats should particularly be involved in the operation, maintenance and management of water infrastructure/facilities at appropriate levels progressively, with a view to eventually transfer the management of such facilities to the user groups/local bodies. When it comes to implementation the tilt is more towards privatization rather than giving it to the Local Bodies, despite the fact that some States, notably Tamil Nadu and Karnataka, have proved and have taken the lead in successfully demonstrating the capabilities of local bodies in managing water resources and services.

## Conclusion

The official moves of the WTO or the GATS (General Agreement on Trade in Services) could not be pinned down with citation as cause for all these cases, at least in India, but for the explicit citation one can make about the investments made in this business through FDI. It can be spoken in terms of trading and investment defining water as a commodity and not in terms of water distribution service as such on a large scale. It has all the evidence – a few explicit and some tacit—to prove that the culture radiated by globalization and lack of power and competence at the local body level that have brought about concern over stealing community water for private profits while a section of the traditional rural community starve for water. The grassroots institutions created through the Constitutional Amendment (73rd Amendment to the Constitution of India) with the sense of commitment are able to manage water and distribute the same to the people as entitlements of people. Decentralisation provides opportunity to protect and manage natural resource for the benefit of the communities. How the above opportunity is being used depends on the leadership quality of the individuals who assume power.

### REFERENCES

A Review of Public-Private Partnership in Water and Environmental Sanitation in India , New Delhi: DFID (1999).

A Vaidyanathan, Tanks of South India, Centre for Science and Environment, New Delhi, 2001.

A. Agarwal and S. Narayan, 2002. Making Water Everybody's Business. The Centre for Science and Environment, New Delhi.

Advocacy Internet: Stealing our Water – Implications of GATS for Global Water Resources.

Ashim Goyal: 'Getting Water from Public-Private Partnership' India Infrastructure Report 2004.

Barlow Maude, "Blue Gold – The fight to stop the corporate theft of the World's Water" New Press, April 2003.

Bhagwathi Jagdish, In Defense of Globalisation, Oxford Publication, Chennai.

Central Ground Water Board (2003) Dynamic Groundwater Resources of Tamil Nadu, GoI.

Department of Evaluation and Applied Research (2002) Tamil Nadu – An Economic Appraisal, 1999-2000, GoTN.

Department of Municipal Administration and Water Supply (2202) Policy Note, GoTN.

Dina Malar (Tamil Daily) January 27, 2006 reports that the wife of the former Village Panchayat President, Kamsan has filed a case against the South India Bottling Company that the company people took Kamson to a tourist resort in Coutralam and gave him a lethal cocktail of drinks so as to get the no objection certificate. Mr Kamson who recently recovered from jaundice died after returning from the cocktail party.

Dina Malar (Tamil Daily) January 27, 2006.

Gangaikondan Panchayat President dies in Hospital, The Hindu, August 31, 2005.

Government of Tamil Nadu G.O. MS No.260 RD (WSI)dated 9th Dec.1998.

Government of Tamil Nadu, 1994, The Tamil Nadu Panchayats Act.

Institute of Water Studies (1998) State Framework Resources Plan for Tamil Nadu, Government of Tamil Nadu.

Institute of Water Studies (2003) "River Conservation and Management Issues" GoTN.

J. Raja Chelliah, Global and Local – Newsletter, RGC-GRI, Gandhigram.

J. Raja Chelliah, Global and Local, News Letter, RGC-GRI, Gandhigram.

Jagdish Bhagwati, In Defense of Globalisation (Oxford University Press, 2004).

*Jayaraman Nityanand, Water Wars and Bottle Battles, India Resource Centre, May 24, 2005* www.IndiaResource.org.

Keith Gauntlett, 'Water – Life Before Profit' Integral Liberation Vol.9, No.2 June 2005.

Keith Gauntlett, 'Water – Life Before Profit' Integral Liberation Vol.9, No.2 June 2005.

Lyla Mehta and Birgit Ia Cour Madsen, Poor People's Access to Water, IDS Bulletin 35.1.

M R Rajagopalan, Global and Local, Newsletter, RGC-GRI, Gandhigram.

M. Mehta (1999) A Review of Public – Private Partnerships in Water and Environmental Sanitation in India, New Delhi: DFID.

Narsalay Raghav, Who Controls Rights over Water in an Unfolding GATS Regime? June 2003

National Water Development Agency (2000) Inter-basin Water Transfer Proposals, GoTN.

New Tirupur Area Development Corporation Limited, Minister for Information, Publicity and Local Administration.

Policy Note 2005-2006 Government of Tamil Nadu, NTADCL.

Policy Note, Government of Tamil Nadu, 2001-02.

Public Works Department (1994) Groundwater Resources of Tamil Nadu – Present Status of Development, GoTN.

Public Works Department, Groundwater Resources of Tamil Nadu – Present Status of Development, GoTN.

Rama, Our Water Resources, (Popular Science Series) National Book Trust, India.

S Kasi Viswanathan, Thamiraparani Thanneer Kollai, July 2005.

S. Viswanathan, "Taking on the Sand Lobby", Frontline, 7th November 2003, pp. 38-40.

*SANDEE Policy Brief: Tank Degradation and Poverty Reduction.* www.dandeeonline.org.

Season and Crop Report of Tamil Nadu 2003-04 p13 Dept. of Economics and Statistics, Chennai.

SIPCOT, Allotment Order for Plots addressed to South India Bottling Co.(P) Ltd. Ref:N.P-1/GKN/SIBCPL/04 dated 21.10.2004.

Soumyen Sikdar, Contemporary Issues in Globalisation, Oxford Press 2005.

Soumyen Sikdar: Contemporary Issues in Globalisation, Oxford Press, New Delhi 2005.

Special Issue on Farmers Conference held on 9.2.2004; Federation for Protection of Water and Livelihood Resources, Karur.

Statement by Dr. Prodipto Ghosh, Secretary, Ministry of Environment and Forests on Water Issues at the Twelfth Session of the Commission on Sustainable Development, April 2004 (published by: Permanent Mission of India to the UN e-mail:india@un.int).

Tamil Nadu State Planning Commission (2003) Balancing Competing Uses and Management - Need for an Ecological Water Resources Policy, GoTN.

The Hindu 9th December 2005.

The Hindu, Thursday, September 29, 2005.

The Hindu, Tuesday May 10, 2005 Cancel License of Soft Drink Unit.

V. R. Krishna Iyer, The Hindu, dated 28.01.2004.

Vandana Shiva, 'The First and Last Commons' Yojana June 2005 Vol.49.

William Nordhaus et al Nature's Numbers: Expanding the National Economic Accounts to include the Environment (Washington, D.C.:National Academy Press, 1999).

www.hinduonnet.com *S Viswanathan, Bottling Thamiraparani (Frontline).*

www.hinduonnet.com *S Viswanathan, Bottling Thamiraparani.*

www.IndiaResource.org *Coca-Cola Linked to Bribery Scandal.*

# 6

# Common Property Resource Management in Panchayati Raj–Status and Opportunities

*V. Ragupathy*

## Common Property Resources: Concept and Definition

Interest in the study of Common Property Resources (CPR) commenced with the publication of a famous article in science in the year 1968 by Garrent Hardin titled 'The Tragedy of Commons'. Hardin strongly argued for the privatization of common natural resources held by the State to save them from environmental degradation or the tragedy of commons[1]. Hardin says that individuals' as self seekers have a tendency to over-exploit common resources and they are not capable of managing common assets collectively among themselves. According to him individual rationality leads to collective irrationality. Individuals will ruin common resources. A number of studies emerged against the theory of Hardin all over the world. Living models of management of common resources by grassroots institutions came into the limelight as an alternative to Hardin's model. Models of community management of resources are found even in the West in Canada and U.S.A.[2] As a result theories are formulated to highlight the importance of grassroots institutions in the management of common property resources. Now the world community shows interest in conserving global commons like the ozone layer, high seas and the Artic Region. Common property resources are considered as the essential and the most fundamental requirement for the survival of our planet.

Even though there are a number of definitions of CPR it is very difficult to give one single definition acceptable to all. One acceptable definition of common property resources is "resources accessible to the whole community to which no individual has exclusive property rights."[3] Common property resources are the resources managed by the community organisations (traditional, modern or elected) for the use of the members of community under certain rules, regulations and restrictions. Common property is not 'no one's property or State property or private property. Modern legal systems can generally understand only two types of property regimes, private property and State property.[4] But in practice a large portion of resources in the traditional societies are still managed by community systems even though these resources may be legally owned by the State.

Villages in India are still rich in common property resources even though they are being fast erroded.[5] Some of the common resources in villages are village tanks, fisheries, grazing lands, thrashing lands, lands, footpaths etc. All these resources are owned by the Government. But the local communities play a critical role in the protection and use of these resources. The State is not able to manage many of these resources spread all over the country without the active initiative, involvement and participation of the local community. Certain resources can be efficiently managed by the local community and no outside agency can manage such resources as efficiently as the locals. Certain resources and communities are totally interdependent and one cannot survive without the other. There is a need for institutions at the grassroots to facilitate community management of common resources. The institutional arrangement can link people with resources. In short common property regimes are forms of management grounded in a set of accepted social norms and rules for the sustainable interdependent use of collective goods such as forests, grazing grounds, fisheries, water resources etc.[6]

## Tradition of Management of Common Property Resources in India

India had a very rich tradition of common property resource management system. Indian villages were functioning as autonomous systems of resource management. Archaeological and literary evidences give a very clear picture of such systems. Karl Marx said that these small and extremely ancient Indian communities were based on common possession of land, on the blending of agriculture and handicrafts.[7] O'Malley remarked that the chief social institutions, as they existed in their integrity, were not individualist but collectivist.[8]

The concept of individual private property in the modern sense was not much acceptable to the traditional Indian village social system. Land, water, forest were treated as resources held in common. Individual families could own and use them within the regulations of the village community .These resources were not considered as commodities which could be sold, purchased or mortgaged without any restrictions.[9] Village community had authority over the resources like land, water; forest, fisheries etc. Village community was collectively responsible for payment of revenue to the State. Community for its survival dependent on the natural resources available locally. They evolved their own traditions and methods for using them in a sustainable way. In areas of settled farming, village typically included not only the cultivated lands but the surrounding village commons, which might include forest, ponds, and pastures. The uses of common resources were governed by customs or by explicit rules.[10] In Tamil Nadu alone there were around 45,000 village tanks managed by local communities. The Uthiramarur inscription gives details of the management of such tanks by the village community[11].

## Decline of Self Governance and of Commons

British conquest of India led to a revolutionary change in the existing resource management system. The British East India Company rule enacted new laws and established the concept of private ownership of land. Lord Cornwallis introduced Permanent Land Revenue System[12]. From that day onwards British economic conceptions for resource management were adopted in India. Suddenly nothing was held in common. The non-land owning class was legally excluded from almost all the traditional rights they enjoyed. The responsibilities of the community over natural resources were taken over by the newly created Revenue Department of the East India Company. The East India Company considered every resource available in India as a tradable commodity. The rights of the community were taken away Bipan Chandra said "The use of pasture and forest lands, irrigation canals, fisheries and homestead plots were some of their rights which were sacrificed."[13] The colonial British Government asserted sovereignty over most of the resources in India, abrogating the traditional rights and management systems of village societies[14]. The Government considered forests as 'timber mines' to be exploited for ship building and railways. Large estates and plantations were promoted for the benefit of private owners sacrificing the traditional rights of the people. The Land Regulation Act of East India Company gave enormous power to State to take land owned or used by the people. This Act is still used to displace people from their land for the purposes of the State. Cultivable land was expanded speedily to increase the land revenue. Even the independent Indian Government, after 1947, did not reverse this process but further extended these trends. According to statistical evidence resources available for common use are fast shrinking.

## Status of Common Property Resources in India and Impact on Rural Poor

The colonial policy of resources management has been recast to the development needs of the economics of free India.[15] Large scale exploitation of resources is getting full support from the Government. Over exploitation of scarce groundwater has been encouraged by distribution of free electricity and subsidised loan facilities for building deep borewells to promote commercial agriculture for the benefit of the industrial sector. Forest areas are transformed into pulp producing farms for the paper industry. India's cultivable land area has been expanded almost to its limit at the cost of common lands. In semi-arid regions the area of commons declined by 30 per cent to 50 per cent between 1950 and 1980.[16]

Still a large section of the population in the village a use one or more CPRs. Particularly women, poor, marginal farmers, widows, destitutes, children and craftsmen are critically dependent on CPR. According to Jodha in States like Rajasthan, Madhya Pradesh, Assam, Manipur, Meghalaya the importance of CPR for the poor is well recorded.[17] In Madhya Pradesh 50 per cent of the labourers and small farmers consume CPR food items. In Rajasthan 30 per cent of the labourers and small farmer households consume CPR food items that are collected or purchased. CPR based income in Rajasthan as proportion of gross income per household is 42 per cent for the vulnerable sections. According to Jodha in many States of India 84 per cent poor rural households collect food items from CPRs. Almost 100 per cent poor household collect fuel, fodder and fibre from CPRs and the average number of CPR based activities per poor rural household range from 3 to 6.[18]

A general observation in Tamil Nadu gives us an clear understanding of the importance of CPRs for the survival of the poor[19]. Majority of the poor households depend on CPRs for their fuel and fodder needs. Women, destitutes and children mostly collect fodder and fuel from CPRs. In case of any difficulty in collecting these items from CPRs it affects these groups critically. Many artisans and craftsmen depend on CPRs for their raw materials like fibre, timber, bamboo, clay, grass etc. Some of the common facilities like common grazing lands benefit not only the entire village but also certain specific sections like cattle rearing communities. In villages people collect house building materials for the construction of their huts and houses from CPRs. Sand, clay, granite, bamboo, grass, agricultural residues are some of the materials once freely available for the poor for construction of their dwellings.

The irrigation tank is the most important common property resource available in most of the villages in Tamil Nadu. In a water starved State like Tamil Nadu, water harvesting is essential for the survival of the rural community.[20] Tamil Nadu had a wonderful tradition of tanks. The community based systems of rain water harvesting in many districts is still functioning. Tanks are useful for irrigation, ground water charging, forestry development, fisheries development etc. It provides fuel and fodder for rural communities. Tank beds are used for cultivation by the landless poor. Short terms crops like cucumber, pumpkin, greens etc. are cultivated in the tank beds in summer. Forestry in tank beds and fisheries in tank water can generate lakhs of rupees for the village community. It is very clear that efficient management of these resources at the local level will bring prosperity to the local community.

**Table 6.1 :** Groups Affected by the Decline of CPRs[21]

| S.No Groups | Impact |
|---|---|
| *(i)* Women | Affected by scarcity of drinking water, non-commercial fodder, fuel, grazing area, non-commercial food items like greens, nuts, vegetables, fruits, tubers etc. Rearing of cattle for additional income becomes more difficult with the decline of grazing lands. |
| *(ii)* Craftsmen | Affected by decline/scarcity /loss of raw materials like bamboo, grass, fibres, wood, clay, sand, minerals etc. |
| *(iii)* Poor, specifically SC/ ST | Affected by decline/scarcity /loss of materials, required for food, fuel, fodder, housing materials, grazing land etc. |
| *(iv)* Marginal farmers | Affected by decline of ground water, neglect of irrigation systems, inability to maintain cattle depending on CPRs etc. |

## Institutional Framework for Self-Governing Institutions for Management of Commons

Hardins theory of Tragedy of Commons and the game theory of Prisoners Dilemma explain the need for institutional arrangements for the management of commons.[22] Without strong institutional arrangements common resources can not survive and they will become open access resources[23]. In such a situation common resources will be over exploited, misused and destroyed. Ostrom[24], Runge[25] and Wade[26] argue that participatory institutions have better capacity than the State machinery to manage common resources at the grassroots. Particularly local resources like irrigation tanks, minor forests, fisheries and common lands can be managed well by local participatory institutions. Olson and Ostrom explain the key determinants of the success of self-governing institutions for the management of common resources. Olson suggests that self- governing small groups are able to generate collective action for common good.[27]

The design principles of Ostrom are useful in understanding the working of participatory institutions for the management of commons. Ostrom has studied self-governing participatory institutions for the management of common property resources in many parts of the world. She could find some key determinants of success of the participatory institutions.[28] Some of them are listed hereunder :

(1) The size of the organisation must be small.
(2) The organisation must have simple rules known to most of the members of the organisation.
(3) Members must have control over the management of the ogranisation.
(4) Members must have the capacity to regulate the behaviour of each other in relation to the management of the organisation.
(5) Members must be given assurance by the organisation that their contributions will be proportionately rewarded.
(6) The benefits of the collective action must be equitably shared.
(7) The violators of the rules of the organisations must be proportionately punished.

(8) The rights of the members to make operational decision must not be challenged by any external government agencies.

(9) Government must allow the organisations to function with reasonable independence.

(10) Ostrom's design principles help to understand the efficiency of various types of participatory institutions at the grassroots. Particularly they are very useful to study the working of institutions like Panchayati Raj Institutions, self-help groups, user organisations and traditional community-based organisations.

## Status of Institutional Arrangements for Management of Common Property Resources

Some models of management of common property resources at the grassroot level are available. Generally they can be classified in to the following types :

*(i)* Traditional community-based systems of management.
*(ii)* Participatory system of users promoted by external non-governmental agencies and governmental agencies.
*(iii)* Elected village panchayats.[29]

Traditional community-based systems of CPR management in villages are working all over the country. Inspite of modernisation and State intervention some of the traditional systems are still efficient and powerful. In certain areas, where resources are scarce and critical for the life of the people, these systems operate efficiently. Particularly irrigation systems are managed by traditional arrangements in many parts of the country. Even though these systems are efficient, generally they are not based on the principle of equity. The traditional CPR systems are mostly influenced by caste considerations. The rich and powerful can easily manipulate the system for their benefit. Weaker sections like scheduled castes, scheduled tribes, women find it difficult to participate in the management of CPRs on equal terms with the higher caste people. The traditional system could not accommodate the aspirations of these sections.

In recent times NGOs and Government agencies are promoting participatory management of natural resources. A joint forest management model under social forestry programme is promoted by the Government directly or through NGOs.[30] The Sukuomajri model promoted in Chandigarh, the Van Panchayat model in Uttar Pardesh and the Pani Panchayat in Maharashtra are good examples of such ventures.[31]

The Government or non-Government agencies sponsored CPR management models may not be appropriate for the entire country. These agencies have their own limitations and do not have the capacity to manage the resources throughout the country. Their activities are restricted to only certain pockets and certain types of resources. Panchayati Raj is the system available for CPR management all over the nation. The democratic structure of Panchayati Raj ensures people's participation to a great extent. It also facilitates the participation of SCs, STs and women in the decision-making process at the grassroots.

## CPRs under the New Panchayati Raj System

The 73rd Constitutional Amendment Act has included 29 subjects in 11th Schedule (Article 243 G). The State Panchayat Acts have also give certain responsibilities to Panchayati Raj Institutions. Based on these Acts Panchayats can deal with the following CPR related activities :

(a) Irrigation Tanks
(b) Supply Channels
(c) Water Harvesting Schemes
(d) Land Development and Soil Conservation
(e) Fisheries Development

(f) Minor Forest Development
(g) Social Forestry and Farm Forestry
(h) Drinking Water
(i) Fodder
(j) Fuel
(k) Non-conventional Energy Resources
(l) Agricultural Development
(m) Grazing Lands
(n) Threshing Grounds
(o) Cattle Sheds
(p) Cart Stands
(q) Tubewells
(r) Environment Protection
(s) Community Assets.

The above mentioned subjects are critical for the rural economy in the rural areas. The activities of the Village Panchayats can be focussed around important CPRs. As per the new Panchayati Raj System, Village Panchayats have the responsibility of protecting, developing and making them available for the benefit of the entire community based on the principle of equity. Common Property Resources are mostly uncared for in many villages in the absence of any political device available for people to participate in their management in a systematic manner. The creation of strong democratic structures through Panchayati Raj System paves way for people's participation in the management of CPRs. Village Panchayats have enough powers and resources not only to maintain the traditional CPRs like irrigation tanks, unclassified forest, threshing grounds but also modern CPRs like community shelters, public toilets, hand pumps etc. Large scale funding by the Central and State Governments can be judiciously used for the development, maintenance and repair of CPRs by Panchayats.[32]

Some of the resources which are common to more than one Village Panchayat have to be jointly managed by the concerned Village Panchayats. Some of the bigger resources like irrigation channels, forests, roads, mines, river beds can be managed by the District Panchayat or Mandal Panchayat.

## Gram Sabha and Common Property Resources

The Gram Sabha in a Village Panchayat has a significant role to play in the management of common property resources under the control of the Village Panchayats. It provides an opportunity to the entire voting population of the Village Panchayat to sit together to discuss the problems affecting the village commons.[33] CPRs like water, fuel and fodder land are the priority items in many villages. The Gram Sabha will be a valuable device for the villagers to decide issues on matters affecting their day-to-day life and survival. So there is a great scope for CPR to become the focal point for deliberations at the Gram Sabha meeting. Particularly women and other marginal sections like SC/ST will take CPRs as a very sensitive issue. The scope for micro-level planning and participatory development has increased with the introduction of the new Panchayati Raj System. In the new system from village to district level most of the development programmes will be under the control of the people's representatives. Even some of the progressive resource management programmes like land reforms are also included in the 11th Schedule (243G) of the Constitution. In States like West Bengal even tubewells used by farmers are under the control of the Village Panchayat as per the State Panchayati Raj Act.

The Gram Sabha ensures transparency in the activities of Village Panchayats. Open debates in front of the community increase the accountability of the leaders to the people. The already functioning traditional community meetings in villages give hope for people's participation in the Gram Sabha. Once transparency and accountability are ensured, there is more scope for people's participation. So far people do not have any legal power device to control the administration of CPRs at the grassroots level. The constitutionally created Gram Sabha, for the first time, provides people an opportunity to bring the affairs of village level administration under their direct control. A powerful element of direct democracy has been introduced at the village level by the new system. In this changed system, there is great scope for participatory management of CPR on the principle of equity. Valuable resources like irrigation tank, ground water, forest lands, grazing lands, mineral resources etc. will be efficiently managed for sustainable use.

## Strengthening of Panchayats for Managing Commons

In many States, particularly in States like Tamil Nadu, Panchayats are still functioning as agencies of Government and they are motivated to implement only the schemes, programmes and policies of Central and State Governments.[34] Panchayats are more influenced by the Government than the local community. So Panchayats are not able to emerge as self-governing participatory institutions. 73rd Constitutional Amendment and Article 243G of the Indian Constitution expect Panchayats to play a key role in the management of critical common natural resources at the grassroots. But still most of the State Governments are not ready to transfer the management of these resources to Panchayats. Most of the laws and rules introduced by the East India Company and British government are still in force.[35] State Governments should take steps to transfer some of the local resources like irrigation tanks, common lands and fisheries to Panchayats and remove the existing strings of controls. States should provide incentives to Panchayats for the efficient management of natural resources. Natural resources are great assets and they can generate income to Panchayats which can become more self-sufficient by developing local natural resources. These resources, if managed efficiently, can play a significant role in the reduction of poverty and the creation of livelihood opportunities. Resources like irrigation tanks will be better managed by the stakeholders. So Panchayats can permit user groups to manage these resources under the control of Panchayats. A variety of minor minerals are available in rural areas. These resources are exploited on a large scale by outside agencies and it is a threat to the local ecological balance.[36] Particularly sand mining has emerged as a threat to the livelihood of the people. Panchayats must be given powers to regulate the mining of minor minerals in their area.[37] Panchayats have the responsibility to protect the local ecology and the State should not take away the power of Panchayats to protect the local eco-system. Maximum possible efforts must be taken by the State to promote the use of natural resources locally. Local users, craftsmen and local industries must get local rural raw materials at a lower price as an incentive. In recent years local people are denied their rights to use the local resources.[38] Licences and permits to exploit these resources are given to outside commercial agencies by the State Government. As a result poor farmers and craftsmen are denied their traditional rights to use the local resources for their livelihood. If Panchayats are given sufficient powers, the interests of the local users can be protected. The local community will have more interest in protecting the resources like water bodies, forests and common lands, if they get direct benefit from these resources.[39]

## Conclusion

The natural resource capital of this country cannot be sustainably developed without the participation of the mass of people through grassroot level action and the effective institution available for such mass action is Panchayati Raj. Unless the environment and resources are monitored, protected and developed at the village level no macro level government programme at the national level can save this country from starvation and decay. As Dr. M.S. Swaminathan says "Business and industry by and large adopt a short-term view with reference to the exploitation of natural resources. Our life support systems are in distress and there is little political interest in making scientific land and water use mandatory. The emergence of Panchayati Raj and Nagarapalika institutions may provide an opportunity for adopting a new land and water ethic, provided there is political will for their ecological empowerment".[40] The Panchayat and the Gram Sabha have given an opportunity to the people to directly participate in the decision-making process and there is a great scope for the revival of the common property resource management state. Non-governmental agencies, activists and other public interest groups must motivate people to successfully use this opportunity to protect the CPR for their own benefit.

## NOTES

1. Gauent Hardin, and Jhon Baclen (Eds.), *Managing the Common,* New York: W.H. Freeman and Company, 1977.
2. Berkes Firkert (Ed.), *Common Property Resources,* Dehradun: International Book Distributors, 1991.
3. N.S.Jodha, "Common Property Resources and Rural Poor in Dry Regions of India", *Economic and Political Weekly,* XXX,27, 5th July 1986.
4. Kanchan Chopra, Gopal K. Kadekodi, M.N. Murlhy (Eds.), *Participatory Development, People and Common Property Resources,* New Delhi: Sage Publications, 1990.
5. Rural off Farm Common Property, Business Line, Madras, (26th December,1994), p.14.
6. Berkes Firkert (Ed.), Op.cit
7. Engels Marx, *The First Indian War of Independence 1857-58,* Moscow: Progressive Publishers, 1988, p.15.
8. Cited in A.R. Desai, *Social Basis of Indian Nationalism,* Bombay, Popular Prakashan, 1982, p.13.
9. Ibid.
10. Business Line, Op. cit.
11. K.A.,Nilakanta Sasthri, *The Cholas,* Chennai: University of Madras, 1994.
12. Bipin Chandra, *Modern India,* New Delhi: National Council for Education Research and Training, 1982, p.102.
13. Ibid.
14. Ibid.
15. M. Gadgil, and R.Guha., *This Fissured Land: An Ecological History of India,* New Delhi: Oxford University Press 1997.
16. Jodha N.S. Op. cit.
17. Ibid.
18. Ibid.
19. V. Ragupathy, *Participatory Management of Natural Resources: Irrigation Tanks in Panchayats,* New Delhi: Concept Publishing Company: 2004.
20. Ibid.

21. V. Ragupathy, Common Property Resource Management in Panchayati Raj in Palanithurai G.(ed), *Empowering People : Issues and Solution*, New Delhi : Concept Publishing House, 1996, p,100
22. G.Hardin, Op.cit.
23. Ibid.
24. E.Ostrom, *Governing the Commons: Evolution of Institutions for Collective Action*, New York: Cambridge University Press, 1990.
25. C.F. Runge, "Institutions and Freeridders: The Assurance Problem in Collective Action," *The Journal of Politics*, 46/1 1984
26. R.Wade, *Village Republics – Economic Conditions for Collective Action in South India*, Bombay: Orient Longman, 1987.
27. M. Olson, *The Logic of Collective Action: Public Goods and the Theory of Groups*, Cambridge: Harvard University Press, 1973.
28. E Ostrom, Op.cit.
29. V. Ragupathy, Op.cit.
30. Kanchan Chopra, Gopal K. Kadekodi, M.N. Murlhy (Eds.) Op.cit.
31. *Ibid.*
32. V. Ragupathy, Op.cit.
33. G. Palanithurai, V. Ragupathy, *Functional Efficiency of Gram Sabhas in Tamil Nadu*, New Delhi: Concept Publishing House, 2006.
34. G. Palanithurai, *New Panchayati Raj System at Work: An Evaluation*, New Delhi: Concept Publishing Company, 1999.
35. M. Gadgil, and R.Guha, , *This Fissured Land: An Ecological History of India*, New Delhi: Oxford University Press, 1997.
36. Ibid.
37. G. Palanithurai, *Pathfinders Series Number-9*, Gandhigram: Rajiv Gandhi Chair for Panchayati Raj Studies, 2006.
38. M. Gadgil, and R.Guha, Op.cit.
40. M.S.Swaminathan, "Population and Food: A Crisis on the Horizon, *Survey of the Environment*, Madras: The Hindu, 1994.

# 7

# Social Liberation and Empowerment in Panchayats— Stages and Struggles in Tamil Nadu

*V.Ragupathy*

Aspiration for social liberation and empowerment at the grassroot has been triggered by the 73rd Constitutional Amendment Act and the policy of reservation of positions for SC, ST and women in Panchayats. In a feudal rural society where inequity is institutionalized, democratic decentralization has little meaning without affirmative action. Some of the social revolutionaries like B.R.Ambedkar considered empowering Panchayats without social leveling as a threat to marginalized groups[1]. The Gandhian concept of Gram Swaraj was opposed by Ambedkar and others who considered the village as a sink of localism, a den of ignorance, narrow mindedness and exploitation.[2] More power to Panchayat means more power to high caste, majority community and dominant groups in the villages and it may result in more exploitation of poor minority groups and socially deprived classes.[3] Against this background, 73rd Constitutional Amendment included social justice as one of its main objectives of the Panchayati Raj System. Development without equity does not mean anything to poor. Reservation for women, SC and ST in Panchayats is an important step in the direction of ensuring social justice and equity. Democracy has it's own strength and it gives power to the poor to bargain. Reservation for SC and ST has opened the scope for bringing fundamental change in the power structure by providing right to scheduled caste people to participate in decision-making and governance at the grassroot.

But legislation alone cannot bring social transformation. Many legislations for social transformations could not bring much changes in the society. Numerous laws to improve the status of SC, ST and women have not been properly implemented. According to legal sociologist Upendra Bakshi there are two laws in India i.e.[4] One enacted by the State and the other: societal law. The laws enacted by the legislatures alone could not bring much impact in the society. Some times societal laws are more powerful than the laws of the State. The empowerment of scheduled caste people is a long process of struggle and there are number of stages in it.[5] Empowerment is enhancing an Individual's or groups capacity to make decisions and transform their choices into desired actions and outcomes. Empowerment has to give the capacity to use the available choices and it must bring the desired results. Empowerment also means redressing unbalances of power between those who have it and those who don't.[6] Occupying formal position by a SC person in Panchayats is not sufficient. It necessarily does not empower him. Mere providing positions to SC people in Panchayats is not the end of the empowerment process and it may be only a beginning.[7] There is a need for close study of the process of empowerment of SC people in Panchayat.

Reservation for SC people in Panchayats is a policy of the State and enactment of a law is a step in the legal domain. But implementation of the policy and the process of empowerment takes place in political, social and economic domains. As Upendra Baxi points out the societal and customary laws some times are more powerful in the social domain than the laws of the legislature. It is possible for SC people to contest in elections and occupy positions in Panchayats. But it is still very difficult for them to execute their power. Positions in Panchayats do not bring much changes in the position of the elected representatives in the social and economic domain.

Panchayat is one of the major formal institution in a village. But there are many informal institutions in a village which affect the process of empowerment. In villages cultural practices, traditions and norms play a critical role and economic relationships between different social groups influences the power relationship. The lower level bureaucracy plays a significant role in the functioning of Panchayats and they have their own un-official institutional arrangements in their dealings with Panchayats. Empowerment of SC is very much affected by the lower level administration.

Empowerment is the capacity to make choices and transform these choices into desired actions and outcomes. Reservation alone does not give this capacity. But State does not take sufficient steps to build the capacity of the elected leaders.[9] There is no powerful civil society working for to building the capacity of SC people to use the policy of reservation effectively. In many places the SC people are locked into a cultural framework in which they accept their disempowerment.[10] Very few efforts have been taken to liberate them from this cultural and psychological bondage.

Where they are free from the disempowering psychological lock, social institutions do not allow them to enjoy their equal status. When SC leaders are ready to function on their own, they have to face the challenges of the existing rural social institutions. Economic status of SC representatives plays a very significant role in the process of empowerment. Assets give them the capacity to aspire and struggle. Assetless people find it very difficult to struggle for their empowerment. Reservation policy must be followed by building the capacity of the SC people and efforts to bring a favourable change in the existing social and administrative institutional structures at the grassroot in the absence of such efforts empowerment will not deliver the desired outcomes.[11]

## Empowerment Process in Panchayats in Tamil Nadu

Against this backdrop the status of the process of empowerment of scheduled caste people in Panchayats in Tamil Nadu is discussed. Tamil Nadu is considered as a progressive State with a long history of struggle for social liberation. Non-Brahmin movement since

1920 worked for reservation policy in legislature and Government offices. The Anti-brahminical movement in Tamil Nadu headed by E.V.Ramasamy Periyar contributed significantly for the development of non-Brahmins and backward communities. Many social legislations have been passed in Tamil Nadu for the social and economic upliftment of backward communities. Compared to many States Tamil Nadu has made significant achievements in the areas of social development. Powerful civil society organisations are functioning and working for the empowerment of weaker sections. But few scholars think non-Brahmin movement could not bring any significant changes in the status of SC people in Tamil Nadu, it gave more power to backward communities and it did not ensure the upward mobility of SC people.[12]

## Struggle for Social Justice

The policy of reservation for SC and ST in Panchayats has brought changes in the rural power-structure in Tamil Nadu. The positions reserved for SC people in Panchayats have been filled as per the law in the 2006 elections. Nearly one third of the positions in Village Panchayats have been occupied by SC/ST elected representatives. In Tamil Nadu out of 12,593 Village Panchayats Presidents 3,810 Presidents are from SC and 237 Presidents are from ST.[13] The numerical strength of SC elected representatives in Panchayats is very impressive. It is possible for such a strong group of SC Panchayat representatives to bring social justice at the grassroot. They have the critical mass to bring a social transformation.

But the experiences of SC representatives in Panchayats reveal that the process of empowerment of SC people through Panchayats has to face many challenges difficulties and hurdles. Even though SC people form about 19 per cent of the population in Tamil Nadu, they have not still emerged as a political force. SC population is thinly spread all over Tamil Nadu and only in few pockets they are numerically strong. They are everywhere but everywhere they are minority. They are also disintegrated into many caste groups. There is no unity among different SC caste groups. Each caste group has it's own political outfit and they are in conflict with each other.

Even in reserved Panchayats, SC people are not able to influence the electoral outcome. Other caste groups normally unite together and prevent the ascendancy of SC power in villages. In most cases the other backward castes put puppet SC candidates. In Tamil Nadu, Village Panchayat elections are not contested on party basis. In the absence of political parties caste play the determining role in the out come of elections and formation of power structure. Caste, clan and hamlet are the vital elements in the electoral process in Panchayats.

In 1996 Panchayat elections it was reported in three village Panchayats of Madurai district the reservation policy of the constitutional amendment was sabotaged. In three Village Panchayats, where President's office was reserved for SC no one was allowed to contest by local community. From 1996 to 2005 in spite of the repeated attempts by State Election Commission the process of election in the three Panchayats were not permitted to complete. It was reported that in many districts of Tamil Nadu elected SC leaders were not permitd to function by the dominant local community.[14] After the first Panchayat elections few SC elected Panchayat representatives were brutally murdered. In this context the need for deeper understanding of the process of empowerment of SC in Panchayats is very much required.[15]

## Empowerment in Practice

Process of empowerment is not one quantum jump. As Baviskar argues one does not jump from a zero power situation to all power situation.[16] Bavishkar argues that empowerment has several stages and it is a long journey. But it is not necessary that every individual or group should pass through all these stages. Depending upon the existing situation the empowerment process takes place. Stage here means the situation in which an elected representative has to operate. Based on the experience in Tamil Nadu five stages could be identified in the process of empowerment of Scheduled Caste Presidents in Panchayats. In few villages of Tamil Nadu SC people were prevented from using legitimate right to contest in Panchayat elections for reserved positions. Even elected Presidents are prevented from using symbolic powers. Particularly in certain pockets of Madurai, and Virudhunagar district this situation was noticed. In villages where SC people are very few and caste discriminations are very high. SC people find it very difficult to contest in Panchayat elections. So they do not contest in elections. The five identified stages are discussed here.[17]

**Table 7.1** : Empowerment Leader

| Sl. No. | Stages of Empowerment |
|---|---|
| 1. | Rejection |
| 2. | Tokenism |
| 3. | Compromise |
| 4. | Struggle |
| 5. | Empowerment |

## Rejection

The powerful middle and upper caste groups are not able to accept the policy of reservation. For these groups their caste and customary norms are superior than the laws of the State. Low level of awareness is one reason for this status. These groups generally try to sabotage any measures for social transformation in rural areas. Powerful caste groups do not allow the SC people to rear the benefit of the policy of reservation. SC people are threatened and prevented from contesting elections. Even if they are elected they are forced to resign. In some cases even elected representatives are murdered. The SC elected leaders are prevented from attending their official duties. They are humiliated. They are forced to follow the directions of the majority community.[18]

Particularly in Panchayats where the non-SC caste groups are in majority they feel that they have the natural right to occupy positions in Panchayats and the policy of reservation of seats for SC is a violation of natural justice. Absence of the role of civil society organisations in convincing these groups on the intentions of the policy of social justice is another reason for this state of affair. In Tamil Nadu major political parties also do not come forward to take any bold steps to challenge and correct this dangerous trend. Because in villages the dominant caste groups have very big vote bank major political parties are not ready to come forward to support the cause of scheduled caste people in Panchayats. Even though this is a problem related only to so few Panchayats, there is scope for the problem to spread to other areas.

## Tokenism

Tokenism is doing something in insincere way so as to be seen to be obeying the law or satisfying a particular group of people. Tokenism is more dangerous than rejection. In rejection it is openly declared that the reservation policy is not acceptable. But in Tokenism the reservation policy is manipulated to satisfy the needs of the powerful groups.[19] In majority of the reserved Panchayats in Tamil Nadu the policy of Tokenism is practiced. Caste groups and powerful individuals manipulate the electoral process and elect reliable candidates as Presidents and members. They control Panchayats by proxy. The elected leaders are powerless and helpless. Any work related to Panchayats and all their powers are enjoyed by somebody else.

Tokenism is practiced generally where SC people are in minority and organisations working for SC people are not active. Particularly where powerful caste groups are not able to reject the policy of reservation they try to practice Tokenism. It allows them to enjoy power without responsibility. In this situation the SC leaders are not in a position to bring any changes in the existing social structure. They could not improve the status of Scheduled Caste people in their Panchayats.

## Compromise

When Tokenism is not possible, powerful caste groups try to accommodate SC leaders in the Panchayats. When SC people have reasonable awareness and considerable population in the Panchayat area powerful caste groups want to come to an understanding with SC leaders. In many places the SC candidates for the election are nominated after due consultation with majority caste groups. Particularly when SC people are disunited powerful caste groups use the opportunity to accommodate SC candidates of their choice in Panchayats. Independent SC candidates are defeated by the powerful caste groups by using this method. Even though elected SC leaders are not the puppets, they are dominated by the powerful caste groups. The SC Panchayat leaders can not take decisions on their own. Social reality compels the SC Presidents and members to practice this as a method of compromise.[20] Most of the SC Presidents are economically and socially marginalized and they find it very difficult to fight with powerful groups. Instead they take a position of compromise. Such leaders are not able to bring any change in the existing social structure.[21] But some times they may be effective in implementing welfare schemes for the benefit of the Scheduled Caste people.

## Struggle

Struggle is a very significant stage in the process of empowerment. When SC people are economically and politically well placed they are in a position to assert and struggle for their legitimate rights. Particularly in Panchayats, where SC people are in numerically strong there is a tendency to assert their rights. The political parties, NGOs and Dalit organisations play a critical role in the process of struggle. Once SC are elected, they try to assert their legal rights to use the power to make decisions. In this process there are opportunities to antagonize the powerful caste groups in the village. They are abused and attacked. Most of the Presidents have a non SC Vice-Presidents. Majority of the members are from other communities. There is no reservation in the appointment of

Panchayat Clerks in Tamil Nadu. Panchayat Clerk, a key person in the Panchayat Administration, normally does not facilitate an SC President to function independently. A SC Panchayat President has to convince and get the support of all these forces for effective management of Panchayat. In many cases it leads to violent struggle also. But few SC Panchayat Presidents are able to convince the local community and mobilise support for their activities. In this stage NGOs, civil society organisations and Government agencies must give support to SC leaders. Training, networking and consultancy are very critical in helping the struggling leaders.

## Empowerment

In rare cases in Panchayats empowerment of SC elected leaders has been accepted and SC leaders are able to function freely and independently. SC leaders at this stage are able to make decisions affecting the entire community.[22] In this stage they are able to get the support of other communities for their activities for the development of the Panchayat. It is found that acceptance is possible only under certain conditions. Numerical strength of SC people, level of social development, influence of NGOs and political parties, support structures and leadership play critical role in facilitating acceptance. Particularly in States like Kerala, where social development is high, political parties play a positive role and civil society is active acceptance of SC empowerment in grassroots is very effective and smooth. In Tamil Nadu in rural areas still there is no favourable climate for the empowerment of SC leaders in Panchayats. Panchayat President requires constant support of the members of Village Panchayat and Gram Sabha for effective functioning. Particularly a SC President finds it difficult to get the support of the other groups.

## Case Studies on the Stages of Empowerment

Rajiv Gandhi Chair for Panchayati Raj Studies undertook extensive field research in Tamil Nadu to understand the process of empowerment of women and SC elected Presidents of Village Panchayat.[23] About 200 cases have been studied and analysed.[24] Based on these case studies, five stages in the process of empowerment have been identified. Five cases representing each stage are illustrated and discussed.

## Pappapatti Syndrome – A Case of Rejection

Usilampatti Taluk in Madurai District is known for female infanticide and sabotage of reservation in Panchayats. The three Village Panchayats of Pappati, Keeripatti and Nattarmangalam are not able to function since 1996 because of the problem of reservation of the office of the Panchayat President for SC. Between 1996 to 2001 and 2001 to 2005 as per the constitutional requirement elections were announced every six months. But in first five years no SC candidate came forward to contest in elections. In the second five years, candidate contested in elections, but the elected individuals resigned immediately after their elections.

The villages are dominated by one single Most Backward Caste (MBC), the 'Kallar' community. This caste was notified as a criminal tribe during the British rule. These Village Panchayat are dominated by caste Panchayats and traditional practices. The caste Panchayats are bound by stringent community rules. Most of the members of Kallar community are poor and educationally backward. Due to the effects of the Christian Missionary activities, around fifty years back, education was introduced among them. Kallar community is considered as a sub-group of Thevar community, a pre-dominant community in South and East Tamil Nadu. The overall electoral out come, in around 8 districts of Tamil Nadu is determined by the vote banks of Thevar community.

SC people are minorities in these three Village Panchayats where 80 per cent of the population belong to the Kallar community. These single caste dominant villages have local traditional Panchayats which decide the affairs of the village. Pappapatti has a temple which is considered as very sacred for the

Kallar community of the district. This village is considered as the head village for the entire Kallar community of the region.

Against this background when office of President is there three Panchayat were reserved for SC, there were protests from the Kallars of the region. Kallars considered that reservation of Pappapatti for SC was a challenge to their honour and as a first step to damage their traditional practices. First five years no one was permitted to contest in elections. In the second five years due to pressure from NGOs elections were permitted and few candidates contested in elections. But immediately after elections they resigned.

Inspite of efforts by NGOs the process of elections were not allowed to complete and elected Presidents were not ready to function. Major political parties AIADMK and DMK are not ready to take any serious steps to arrest this problem because of electoral compulsion. They do not want to damage their relationship with the Thevar community. Minor political parties like Communist parties and Dalit political parties tried their level best to solve this problem, but they could not achieve anything. NGOs are not able to change the mindsets of the majority community. In 2007 DMK Government took many steps to facilitate.

Pappapatti syndrome is very dangerous because it may spread to other regions of Tamil Nadu. It is a open challenge to the Constitution of India and the concept of social justice. Because of the vote bank politics major political parties are not ready to take clear stand on this issues. State Government has no clear policy to stop this trend. Some of the NGOs and political leaders suggested stringent measures like stopping of Government schemes in these three villages. But Government is still not ready to do so. Because of Pappapatti syndrome many Dalit parties demand changes in the electoral system of India. They demand caste-based proportional representation to SC people. Only such a system could help SC people to elect representatives of their choice.

Participation of political parties in Village Panchayat election is another demand from NGOs and Leftist Organizations. Party based elections may play a positive role in situations like this.

Rejection of reservation requires serious study of the problem from constitutional, legal, administrative, social and cultural angles.

## Uthapuram – A Case of Tokenism

Uthapuram is a Village Panchayat in Sedapatti Block of Madurai District. A block official says "Most of the SC Panchayat Presidents are only puppets of the dominant caste organisations of the village." Sedapatti is well known for atrocities against women and scheduled caste people. Uthapuram Village Panchayat has a population of 1800. The Kallar is the majority caste group with 1100 population and there are 350 scheduled caste people in the Panchayat. Rainfed agriculture is the main source of livelihood. The village has only small and marginal farmers and no individual in the village owns more than 10 acres. The majority Kallar community is classified as the Most Backward Class. Once Kallars were notified as a criminal tribe by the British government. The village has a community Panchayat dominated by the Kallar community. The community Panchayat plays a key role in the affairs of the village, particularly on issues related to the management of common property resources, village temples, festivals and common fund.

When the Uthapuram Village Panchayat President position was reserved for SC women in 1991, a community Panchayat meeting was organised to discuss the issues related to the election. In the meeting it was decided to nominate Chinnu, 45 years old SC widow as the common candidate. She is a landless labourer and uneducated. She has three female children. Her husband was once elected to the office of the President as the common candidate of the village. Her husband was very cooperative and loyal to the community Panchayat.

Chinnu did not know anything related to Panchayat. She was asked to put her signature in the nomination form. The community Panchayats also put two more SC candidates to show the Panchayat elections in the village was free and fair. In three corner contest Chinnu was elected as Panchayat President. But Chinnu was never allowed to sit in the Chair of Panchayat Presidents. The Vice-

President, a man from Kallar community was recognized as the real acting President by the community Panchayat. He functioned as the defacto President of the village. Chinnu never visited the Panchayat office. She was never permitted to attend the meetings of the Village Panchayat. Letters and other correspondences related to Panchayats were not shown to Chinnu. In the cheques she was forced to put her signature and no details were given to her.

She was never allowed to go to Block Office or Collectors Office. She was not permitted to attend training programmes organised by the Government, Chinnu attended farm work to earn her livelihood. She did not have any chance to think about the affairs of the Panchayat. Only benefit she got was the fixed travelling allowance and the sitting fees for attending the Panchayat meetings. Once in a month she went to the house of Panchayat clerk to receive Rs.400. Chinnu is a typical case of tokenism. According to a block official of Sedapatti block most of the SC women Panchayat Presidents are like Chinnu. SC women were used to fulfil the constitutional requirements by the dominant groups.

Presidents like Chinnu are not capable of using their offices because of their social and economic background. They do not have strength to assert their right as elected leaders. Wherever SC are minorities and without economic independence, dominant caste groups never permit them to take their legal role in Panchayati Raj Institutions. They do not have any support structure to facilitate their empowerment. In large number of villages of Tamil Nadu such practices are going on. The constitutional provision of reservation has been satisfied, but the spirit of the Constitution has not been followed.

## Noothulapuram Ms. Kala – A Case of Compromise

Noothulapuram Village Panchayat is located 60 km. away from Madurai city in Dindigul District. It is an industrially backward area and with limited scope for agriculture because of the scarcity of water for irrigation. The population of the village is around 5000. Nearly one third of the population belong to SC people.

Noothulapuram Village is known for conflicts between SC people and non-SC communities. Non-SC communities are dominating the public affairs of the village, particularly in the management of village temples and common property resources. SC people are not permitted to take part in many of the rituals in temple festivals. They have to stand outside, they are not permitted to enter into the temple. Every year temple festival only created further scopes for conflicts between SC and other communities.

The Presidents position was reserved for SC women when the new system was introduced in 1996. The Village Panchayat has it hamlets and Noothulapuram is the biggest among them. When election was announced in 1996 three SC women candidates contested in election. M. Kala, a 10th passed SC women came forward to contest in election. She is a trained health worker. Before election she was working as a field health organizer with Association of Sarva Seva Farms (ASEFA) a leading Gandhian non-governmental organization in Tamil Nadu. She was also associated with Congress Party. Her husband is an ex-service man and a taxi operator. Her family has good reputation in the village. Kala could get non-SC votes also. Because of the support of the non-SC voters Kala could win the election. She was known as a moderate leader and could get the support of other Backward Class voters also. Kala was considered as a candidate of compromise by non-SC communities. The SC youths of the village were very much against the influence of the upper castes in Panchayat administration. But Kala did not want any violent conflict in the village. She wanted to bring peace in the village. Understanding between Kala and dominant community leaders became inevitable. In this process Kala got the displeasure of the SC youths. SC youths considered Kala as the agent of upper caste. But an objective observation reveals that Kala took a pragmatic stand to avoid conflict and violence in the village. Most of the members of the Village Panchayat are from non-SC communities, Vice-President is from the dominant community. In this situation Kala has no option but to come to an understanding with the powerful leaders of various caste groups.

There was no unity among the members of the SC community and so Kala could not depend only on them.

But Kala is very particular that all the funds allocated for the development SC people must be properly used for the benefit of the SC people. She could get all basic facilities to the SC colonies of the Village Panchayat. At the same time she also took all the required steps to fulfil the needs of the other communities. She took pain to convince the non-SC people about the activities of the Panchayat. Kala is case of accommodation. The dominant caste groups found Kala as a candidate of compromise. She was not a proxy Panchayat President. But at the same time she was also not independent. She did not question the authority of the dominant community leaders in some significant areas like temple management and management of common property resources. Because of this she got the displeasure of the SC youths. But at the same time Kala sincerely took all efforts for the development of SC people of the Panchayats.

**Pottuluppatti Mani – A Case of Struggle**

Pottuluppatti is a Village Panchayat in Usilampatti Panchayat Union of Madurai District. Usilampatti is known for the practice of female infanticide and violence against SC people. Pottuluppatti Village Panchayat has a population of 2300. The Village Panchayat has 1,108 voters. Out of them 356 are SC voters. There are six ward members in the Panchayat. Two ward members are from SC. Pottuluppatti Village Panchayat President position was reserved for SC women as per the rules in 2001 Panchayat elections.

In 2001 elections two SC women candidates contested for the post of Village Panchayat President. They were from two different hamlets of the village panchayat and got the support of community of their respective hamlets. Mani, aged 37 contested in the election for the first time with the support of the dominant caste group of her hamlet. Mani was educated upto fourth standard and she was an agricultural labourer. In Panchayat elections candidates have to spend money. Local community leaders gave voluntary contributions to Mani for the election purpose. About Rs.16,000 was spent on election by Mani and the electoral expenses were managed by one Mr. Jeyaraj belonging to a dominant caste. Mani could win the election, with the support of the local community leaders. One of the ward members Mr. Ravi Chandran was elected as the Vice-President by the ward members of the Village Panchayat. He was from the dominant community. He wanted to control the Panchayat using Mani as a Proxy President. As per the rules of the Tamil Nadu Panchayat Act Vice-President plays a critical role in the functioning of Village Panchayat. Bank accounts are jointly operated by the President and Vice-President.

As Mani had studied only upto fourth standard initially she could not understand the administrative procedures of the Village Panchayat. She was influenced by the Vice-President in Panchayat administratoin. She consulted the village elders of all communities. The Village Panchayat got Rs. 1,00,000 for the repair of houses affected by floods. Using the ignorance of the President, the Vice-President and Panchayat clerk got her signature in the cheque and took Rs.30,000 from the amount sanctioned for the repair of houses of SC people. But Block Development Officer could understand the problem and instructed Mani to be careful in future. He instructed the Vice-President and Panchayat clerk to distribute the sanctioned amount to the real beneficiaries without any future delay.

After this, Mani could understand the intention of the Vice-President and tried to assert her power. She wanted to function independently. She activated the village panchayat council and Gram Sabha. Few of the dominant community leaders did not like the change in the behaviour of the Panchayat President. They insisted that she should function as per the instruction of the Vice-President and dominant community leaders. But Mani conducted Village Panchayat ward members meetings and took decisions—she could get the support of four members out of the six ward members. The Vice-President and the another member did not cooperate with the President.

One day when Mani and her family members went to the nearby town, her hut was looted and her thatched hut was burnt by the henchmen of the Vice-President and few of the dominant community leaders. Mani made a complaint in the police. But the police did not arrest the culprits. After a week, few of the dominant caste group attacked Mani and prevented her from entering into the Panchayat office. She could not enter into the office for few days. Again she made a complaint to the police, with the help of the police, she could enter the Panchayat Office. One day when she was conducting the Panchayat meeting, a supporter of the Vice-President from the dominant caste entered into the office and disturbed the meeting. He verbally accused the President. He pulled the saree and the blouse of the President. He physically attacked her. But few of the public came to the rescue of the Panchayat President and protected her.

She went to the District Collector and gave a written complaint against the culprits. She asked for the police protection. Collector ordered from the BDO and the local police to give her enough protection and helped her to discharge her responsibilities without any fear.

Mani went to every family in the village and explained her problems. She asked their help to run a honest and efficient administration in the village panchayat. In the next Gram Sabha meeting she discussed the problems and many of the Gram Sabha members expressed their support to Mani. A Village Panchayat council meeting was called and a resolution to dismiss the Vice-President was passed. The district administration facilitated the implementation of the resolution as per the procedure and the Vice-President was dismissed. With support of the four ward members she could manage the affairs of the Panchayat smoothly. But she did not feel secure and afraid of some of the supporters of the former Vice-President. Mani could fulfil all the basic municipal requirements of the people and took steps to improve the facilitates in the SC colonies. New houses for SC people were constructed. Roads, water and sanitation facilities were provided to SC colonies.

She also undertook programmes for the development of the entire Village Panchayat. Water bodies, of the Village Panchayat were desilted with the active participation of local community. A threshing ground was constructed for the use of the farmers of the village. A child care centre was constructed. Group houses were constructed for SC and backward class people below poverty line. In the beginning Mani could emerge as an independent leader only after great struggle. The village society could not accept a SC women as their President. But Mani could assert their legal rights and she suffered in the process. But she proved that after the struggle she could emerge as an independent leader.

## Kuthambakkam Elango – A Case of Empowerment

Kuthambakkam Gram Panchayat is in Thiruvallur district. It is located about 40 kms away from Chennai city. The village is well connected with the city due to its large number of industries. The village is rich in agriculture and the lands are well irrigated. But 90 per cent of the land is owned by the upper caste people and most of the SC people are without land. Landless villagers are employed as agricultural labourers, construction workers and factory workers. Few of them are involved in illicit arrack trade and petty criminal activities.

In 1996, the Panchayat elections were announced and the office of the President was reserved for SC. Mr. Elango, an Engineer working with Central Government wanted to use the opportunity to serve the village. So he resigned his job and contested in the elections. During the election he mobilized SC youths behind him and he also could influence the upper caste voters of the village. His family is well respected even by the upper caste people. As the SC has the majority votes, the upper caste people were not in a position to influence the out come of the election. Elango could win the elections with the support of the cross section of the community.

Once Elango was elected he fully asserted his position. As he is well educated, experienced, well connected, no one could undermine his position. But at the same time Elango also wanted to gain the confidence of the non-SC people of the village. He took special interest in participation of all sections of the village in Gram Sabha meeting. He always consulted the village elders and youth groups on various issues related to the development programme of the village. He wanted to make his Village Panchayat as a model Panchayat and bring integrated development to the entire community emerging as a leader of the all sections of the Village Panchayat. He was not identified as a SC Panchayat President. As a scientist he could use science and technology for the development of the village. He brought many model schemes and pilot projects of various government departments and organizations. He brought real change in the mind set of the village community in favour of social transformation. Panchayat has been used to bring many innovative social transformation initiative like Samathuvapuram (equality village scheme of Government of Tamil Nadu which helps people from all castes to live as a single community).

Elango was well educated with rich administrative experience. He developed contacts with few key officials in Government at the State level. He had a clear vision about development of the village. He used the confidence of various sections of the local community. He was identified by others as the leader of the entire village. His village had a strong population of SC people. In this case the entire village community could accepted the leadership of Elango irrespective of his caste background. Elango is a fully empowered leader as he was able to take his own decision and implement them. He brought the desired results with the support of the cross section of the community.

## Key Determinants of Empowerment of SC in Panchayats

Based on the case studies discussed, few key determinants affecting the process of empowerment are identified.[26] Numerical strength of the SC population plays a critical role in effective implementation of reservation policy. In many reserved Panchayats SC are in minorities . Their minority status do not allow them to enjoy real power. In such cases only tokenism is practiced. Puppet SC leaders are elected and they are controlled by the dominant caste groups. Particularly in Gram Sabha meetings SC Presidents find it difficult to get the support of the members of the majority community. Where SC people have numerical strength and they are in majority, SC elected representatives are more powerful.

**Table 7.2 :** Determinants of Empowerment

| Sl. No. | Key Determinants of Empowerment of SC |
|---|---|
| 1. | Numerical Strength |
| 2. | Social Development of the Panchayat |
| 3. | Economical Status of SC Leaders |
| 4. | Leadership Among SC People |
| 5. | Organizations of SC in the Area |
| 6. | Support from NGOs |
| 7. | Role of Political Parties |
| 8. | Unity among SC Sub-groups |
| 9. | Interest of the Government Officials |
| 10. | Affiliation of SC Panchayat leaders (Associations, Network) |
| 11. | Capacity-Building Programmes |

Unity among the SC people is another factor which influence the process of empowerment. In Tamil Nadu the different caste groups within SC people do not have unity and they are fragmented. The dominant caste groups are using this factor and try to divide and rule.

Economic and educational status of SC people also had a great influence in the process of empowerment. When the SC elected leaders are very poor and assetless, they are not in a position to effectively use the opportunities provided by the reservation policy. Poor SC leaders are used by the dominant caste groups. Educated, middle class SC leaders are able to assert their rights and function independently.

Social development facilitates empowerment of SC people. Villages with reasonable social development provide favourable climate for social change and equity. NGOs also play a critical role in bringing a positive social climate favourable for SC empowerment. Social change and awareness can not be brought by legislation alone. It needs powerful social movements. NGOs and civil society organizations play a critical role in bringing such movements for social change. SC Panchayat Presidents supported by NGOs are able to function independently.

Political parties also can play a significant role in the empowerment process. In States like Kerala, where Panchayat elections are contested on party basis SC leaders enjoy real power. But in Tamil Nadu major political parties do not show interest in empowering SC leaders at the grassroot level. Major political parties are not interested in the empowerment process and they are much worried about the votes of the majority community. In few districts of Tamil Nadu left parties support SC Panchayat Presidents and these leaders are more assertive. When SC elected leaders are supported by political parties, NGOs, and associations, they are able to assert their powers. Leaders affiliated with political parties are more powerful than others. It is found that networks of SC leaders provide confidence and support to SC leaders. Members of such networks are in a better position.

## Conclusion

Village Panchayat level elections are conducted not on party basis. Even though this policy has several advantages, this is not helpful in bringing a climate favourable for social change. In the absence of political parties caste is the main consideration in Panchayat elections. SC leaders elected on party basis have chances to get the support of their respective political parties in their functioning.

When SC people are not united because of the problems associated with sub-caste and inner conflicts they are exploited by the dominant groups in the villages. Horizontal and vertical integration of various sub-castes of SC community from grassroots to higher levels is required. Leadership play a key role in the success of reservation policy. Building leadership among SC is an essential requirement. Leadership schools or training institutions for SC leaders must be promoted by the NGOs.

Networking of SC Panchayat leaders from grassroot level to State level will be very much useful for strengthening SC Panchayat leaders. Network gives them self-confidence and self-reliance. Particularly block level networking of SC Panchayat leaders can facilitate them to emerge as an empowered group. The success of Self-Help Groups (SHGs) of women gives a clear picture of the strength of small groups of marginalized people. It promotes the concept of self-reliance. Most of the SC Panchayat leaders are first generation leaders, they do not have any experience in governance. The rules of Panchayat administration are very complex. Rules and Government orders are not available to them. They are not able to understand the complex language of administration. They need consultancy service in day to day administration. NGOs must come forward to establish such consultancy centres at district level.

Government has not taken any steps to strengthen the emerging SC Panchayat leaders. Government can establish help desks at the district level for Panchayats. An experienced official familiar with the problems faced by the SC Panchayat leaders must be posted for this desk. Most of the SC Panchayat leaders are from poor economic background and without any assets. Many of them work in the fields of upper caste landlords. The poverty of SC leaders are used by the powerful groups to control the SC leaders. In Tamil Nadu, there is no salary for Panchayat leaders. Panchayat Presidents have to spend lot of their energy and time in attending works related to Panchayats. They do not have much time to take up any other employment. Particularly honest Panchayat leaders find it difficult to earn for their livelihood. A reasonable monthly salary must be given to SC leaders with poor economic background.

But Panchayats have opened up opportunities for empowerment at the grassroot. For effective use of these opportunities a powerful social movement is required. To certain extent Non-Governmental Organizations are able to mobilize women at the grassroot through Self-Help Groups. The Self-Help Groups experiments have revealed the capacity of the NGO sectors to organize women for social transformation. Government must come forward to use this capacity of NGOs to empower Scheduled Caste people in Panchayats. Empowerment of SC in Panchayats much depend on the status of SC people in social and economic domain also. It is also found that SC representatives with capacity and assets occupy a stronger position and assert their legal rights. State should work to improve the status of SC people in the social and economic domain. Government should take serious initiatives against discriminative practices at the grassroot. Active involvement of civil society organization is very much required there. It should take place as a mass movement.

Empowerment process is affected by the domains in which it takes place social and economic domains in rural areas are not still conducive for empowerment of SC leaders in Panchayats. In Tamil Nadu, State has not taken significant steps in bringing changes in the social and economic domains. The status of SC Panchayat Presidents are much more better in Kerala and West Bengal because of the favourable climate in the political, social and economic domains. State policies and powerful social and political movements for change have created such a climate in these States. In Tamil Nadu and in many other States and civil society have not taken effective steps in this direction. In the absence of such powerful social and political movement reservation policy cannot achieve desired outcomes.

## NOTES

1. AVARD, Panchayati Raj as the Basis of Indian Polity, New Delhi: AVARD, 1962.
2. PRIA, The State of Panchayats – A Participatory Perspective, New Delhi: PRIA, 2001.
3. S. Viswanathan, Dalits in Dravidian Land, Chennai: Navayana Publishing House:, 2005.
4. Upendra Baxi, The Crisis of Indian Legal System, New Delhi: Vikas Publishing House, 1982.
5. Bavishkar, Stages in Empowerment of Marginalized Groups, paper

presented in the National Seminar, Panchayati Raj – an Institution of Development Organized by Shri Ram Centre, New Delhi: March 2005.

6. R. Alsop, M. Bertelsen, and J. Holland, Empowerment in Practice from Analysis to Implementation, Washington DC: The World Bank, 2006.
7. Bavishkar, *op.cit.*
8. Baxi, *Op.cit.*
9. G.Palanithurai, *Dalit Leadership in Panchayats*, Gandhigram: Rajiv Gandhi Chair for Panchayati Raj Studies, 2003.
10. SC (Scheduled Caste) people are traditionally excluded from power in Indian Society. They were disempowered by the social system for thousands of years. Indian Constitution has given equal rights and freedom to all citizens. It has also facilitated affirmative actions like reservation in public offices for Scheduled Castes and Scheduled Tribes. Still because of historical reasons SC people are not able to assert their rights.
11. G.Palanithurai, *Op.cit*
12. Viswanathan, *Op.cit*
13. State Election Commission, *Report on Elections for Local Governments in Tamil Nadu, 2006,* Chennai: State Election Commission, 2007.
14. V.Ragupathy, Working of Panchayati Raj System in Tamil Nadu, paper presented in Institute of Development Studies, Sussex, (29$^{TH}$ July, 2003).
15. The Hindu, Melavalavu Murder, (25th July 1996).
16. Bavishkar, Op.cit.
17. These stages are identified based on the field work of the Rajiv Gandhi Chair for Panchayati Raj Studies, Gandhigram, Tamil Nadu.
18. S. Viswanathan, *Op.cit.*
19. V. Ragupathy, *Op.cit*
20. G.Palanithurai, *Op.cit*
21. V. Ragupathy, *Op.cit*
22. G.Palanithurai, *Evaluation of Process and Performance of Dalit Panchayat Leaders*, New Delhi: Concept Publishing Company, 2005.
23. Ibid.
24. Five cases are drawn from the reports of Rajiv Gandhi Chair for Panchayati Raj Studies, Gandhigram.

# 8

# Self-Governing Water Republics at the Grassroots

*V. Ragupathy*

Tamil Nadu has a rich tradition of self-governing institutions for the management of irrigation tanks. Particularly small rainfed irrigation tanks have been well managed for centuries by local communities. As per Tamil Nadu Panchayat Act, minor rainfed tanks with less than 100 acres of irrigated area are vested with Panchayats.[1] But in practice, Panchayats are not able to effectively generate people's participation for the management of these tanks. But in some districts of Tamil Nadu where tank irrigation is critical for the people, informal local self-governing institutions have been evolved.[2] These institutions are able to generate people's participation without any outside support or intervention and manage tanks efficiently. It gives great hope for academics and policy-makers interested in studying self-governing local institutions for the management of minor irrigation tanks.

There are numerous studies on self-governing community based institutions for common property resource management in many parts of the world. Scholars like Ostrom, based on many empirical studies on self-governing natural resource management systems, have found certain key determinants for the success of self- governing organisations.[3] Restriction of membership of the stakeholders is one of such critical determinants. Members must be permitted to make and unmake operational rules and regulations for the management of their institutions. The violators of the rules must receive graduated sanctions. Exclusion of free riders from the organisation must be possible. Proportional equivalence between the benefits and costs or contributions must be maintained among the members of the group. The rights of the users to design and make their own local institutions are not to be challenged by external Government authorities. If these conditions are met, it is possible for the stakeholders to evolve and manage their own institutions.

Olson helps us to understand the relationship between participation of stakeholders and factors like size of the group, the nature of benefits to the participants and the presence of leaders.[4] Risk and scarcity are the other two important factors.[5] For survival needs people are forced to take collective action to solve common problems like water scarcity and crop failure. The need for assurance giving institutions is insisted upon by scholars like Olson and Hardin.[6] Many self-governing local organisations in Sivaganga district for tank management fulfil most of the above mentioned conditions.

## The Invisible Water Republics and Local Citizenship in Sivaganga District

A study in Sivaganga district on the management of common property resources indicates that about 65 per cent of the villages have some form of local governance system for the management of irrigation tanks. More than 2000 small irrigation tanks are managed by local community organisations in Sivaganga district.[7] The cultural ecology of Sivaganga district plays a critical role in shaping the local governance system. David Moose, who studied the irrigation tanks of Sivagangai district, regards the sandy type of soil, scanty rainfall and absence of alternative irrigation sources as the major contributors to the evolution of local institutions of irrigation tank management.[8] The areas of the Sivaganga district having light sandy soil are traditionally called Mankala Nadu (Country with sandy soil). The soil does not have water or moisture retention quality. Moisture is very fast evaporated. Rainfed farming is very difficult. So irrigation is essential for agriculture. Hence construction and maintenance of irrigation tanks becomes a necessity. But the area has only light sandy soil and the risk of tank breach is very high.

During the rainy season the tanks must be constantly watched. Every year tank bunds must be strengthened. Because of these reasons there is a need for institutional arrangements for water management. Because of the soil condition frequent irrigation is required to save the crops. Risk and scarcity plays a critical role in the evolution of little water republics in the district.

## Significance of Tank Irrigation in the District

Sivaganga district has a land area of 4126.5 sq.kms. The rainfall is erratic and the average rainfall is about 933 cm.[9] It receives most of its rainfall from the north-east monsoon from August to November. The major part of the area of the district has sandy soil while a small portion has black soil. Because of the soil condition and shortage of water rainfed agriculture is difficult and water has to be stored in irrigation tanks. Only 31 per cent of the land area is under cultivation. Out of the land under cultivation is 66.33 per cent depends on irrigation tanks. Out of the total irrigated area 86 per cent is under tank irrigation. Only 14 per cent of the land area is under other forms of irrigation like well irrigation and river irrigation.[10]

In Tamil Nadu, the State average of tank irrigation is only 24 per cent. The district has 4597 irrigation tanks. Out of this only 161 tanks are river fed and 4436 tanks are rainfed (96.4%). Out of this 4025 tanks are under Panchayats and only 572 tanks are under the Public Works Department. It means most of the tanks are small in size (below 100 acres).[11]

As per rules rainfed tanks having below 100 acres of irrigated land are classified as Panchayat tanks. The Panchayat Union and Village Panchayats are expected to manage the large number of small tanks. Section 133 of Tamil Nadu Panchayat Act gives the following responsibilities and powers to Panchayats :

(i) The management of turns of irrigation,
(ii) Protection and maintenance of tanks,
(iii) The regulation of distribution of water,

(iv) Execute Kudimaramat ( maintenance by local people),
(v) Levy fee for Kudimaramat for the maintenance of tanks, and
(vi) Management of fishery in the tanks.

But the same section puts innumerable conditions on Panchayats over the management of tanks. The Revenue Department has several ways of controlling Panchayats and Panchayats find it impossible to do any of the above mentioned works.

Panchayats are expected to generate people's participation in development activities. The 73rd Constitutional Amendment Act says Panchayats are self-governing institutions. The eleventh schedule of the Constitution gives a large number of functions to the Panchayats to manage natural resources. But in reality Panchayats are still dependent on the State Government for powers and financial resources. Panchayats are treated like agents to implement Government sponsored programmes and schemes. The Inspector of Panchayats (District Collector) has the power to control the day to day administration of the Panchayats. Because of these reasons Panchayats are not able to generate peoples participation for the management of irrigation tanks. But people depend on irrigation tanks for their livelihood in districts like Sivaganga. People have to make their own local institutional arrangements to ensure their food security. In this context in Sivaganga district most of the villages have evolved their own local institutions for the management of irrigation tanks.

## The Kudi or Local Family Membership System in Villages of Sivaganga District

In most of the villages of Sivaganga district, Ramnad district and Pudukkottai district local community organisations are functioning. The basic unit of the organisation is the Kudi or family. Kudi, in the village, means a family which is residing permanently and which is recognized as a member of the village community.[12]

The Kudi system operates in many villages with minor differences. Generally in a village there are two types of membership. Families having land are considered as farming members (Vivasaya Kudi); families without land are called General Kudi or Podhu Kudi.

Generally Kudi is defined as family (married couple) living in the village at least for one year in a joint family or as a nuclear family. Many villages maintain Kudi register. New members are admitted in the month of September. The farming Kudis are required to contribute cash, grain or labour for the management of irrigation tanks and for the general village fund. The general Kudis are required to contribute for the village general fund only. General Kudis have all the privileges of all the common facilities and resources except a share in the tank water. Farming Kudis get a share in the water in the tank and contribute to the maintenance of the tank.

## Village Assembly

Most of the villages of Sivaganga district have village assemblies. The main tasks of the village assemblies are the maintenance of irrigation tank (Kudi Maramat), sharing of water, managing water scarcity, management of common funds, settlement of disputes, managing of temples, organizing festivals. Tank management is the primary task of the village assembly. Village assembly consists of the eldest males of the Kudis. The village assembly is the policy-making and decision making-body. It takes decisions related to the management of irrigation tanks. Some of the major activities of the village assembly are given below :

## Maintenance of Tank

- Annual maintenance work by the farming families,
- Regulation of desilting of tank bed,
- Maintenance of field channels,
- Clearing the supply channel,
- Preparation of tank bunds,

- Strengthening of tank bunds,
- Removal of encroachments,
- Opening and closing of sluices, and
- Repair of sluices and surplus of weir.

### Generating Resources

Fixing the rate of contributions from Kudis in the form of labour, cash, grain and kind.

- Sale of fishing rights,
- Sale of grazing rights,
- Fines for violation of rules, and
- Receiving gifts.

### Management of Water Supply

- Deciding the cropping pattern based on the availability of water in the tank.
- Drafting the irrigation calendar.
- Appointment of common irrigator.
- Appointment of watch and ward staff.
- Deciding method of irrigation duration and rotation,
- Deciding sharing water in times of water scarcity.

### Settlement of Disputes

- Settlement of disputes over sharing, duration, frequency and violation of water supply.
- Controlling illegal use of water imposing fine and penalties for violation of rules.
- Using common irrigators and watch and ward staff to avoid disputes.
- Emergency functions during floods, protection and repair of tank bunds, supply channel and surplus weir during floods.

### Inter-Village Management System

Many of the tanks of Sivaganga district are system tanks, have common watershed and share water available in a common system of tank watershed. So there is a need for coordination of irrigation management among the cluster of villages. For this purpose in above the villages, a federation of villages is still functioning in Sivaganga district in the name of Nadu or Country. The coordination of the Nadu or Country is vested with the peasant representatives of the villages. This traditional institution plays a critical role in the coordination of water management at the regional level. It also undertakes activities related to common festivals, and settlement of disputes between villages.

### Pulikanmai – A Case Study

To illustrate the working of the above discussed system a case study is given here. Pulikanmai is a village located in Kalayarkovil Block of Sivaganga district. The village is located 2 kms. south-west of Kalayarkovil town and 30 kms. away from the district headquarters.

### Ecological Profile of the Village

The village has red sandy porous soil. The local people call their area Mankala Nadu, which, in Tamil, means sandy soil country. Even after heavy rainswater is not retained in the soil. There is very little groundwater and the available water is mostly saline. The irrigation tank is the only source of irrigation. There is limited scope for rainfed agriculture because of the scarce rainfall and the nature of the soil. The irrigation tank is considered the most valuable resource of the village. Even for drinking water people depend on a well in the tank bed. The irrigation tank of Pulikanmai has 93 acres of irrigated land. The waterbed of the tank is 96 acres. The tank has two sluices or water regulators. The village has three major ponds and two small ponds. Twenty years back one pond was used for getting drinking water. The tank water is used for irrigation for about five months from September to January. In the summer months tankbed is used for grazing. The entire Pulikanmai village is covered by trees. The local community believe that a thick cover of vegetation attracts rain to the area. A large number of peacocks and a variety of birds are spotted in the village area. The supply channels and field channels are maintained well. There are three main supply channels to the Pulikanmai tank and there are numerous streams for the flow of rainwater to the various water bodies of the village.

## Socio-Economic Setting of the Village

The village has a population of 850, out of whom 158 are SC people. The majority of the villagers are Udayar Christians. There are 121 Christian Udayar families, two Maravar families, 32 families of Scheduled Caste, two families of Carpenters, two families of Barbers and three families of Washermen. In total 121 Backward Class, 6 Most Backward Class and 32 Scheduled Caste families live in the village.[13] There are no big landlords in Pulikanmai village. No single individual has more than six acres of irrigated land.

In the tank irrigated area 82 families have land. The 93 acres of irrigated land is distributed among 82 families. The average size of land holding is about 1.25 acres. Small land holdings are common in the village. The smallest land holding is 30 cents.

Among the 32 Scheduled Caste families, 12 families have irrigated land. Other 20 families do not have irrigated land. The landless families work in the nearby town and take up agricultural activities. They also get seasonal work in Pulikanmai itself. During harvest season for agricultural work men get about 15 kg. of paddy/ per day and women get about 10 kgs. of paddy. Each family can get work for about 12 days in the harvest season. Each landless family can get about 300 kgs. of paddy as wages in the harvesting season. It fulfils their food need for about 4 months.

## Kudi and Village Assembly System of Pulikanmai Village for Tank Management

As in many other villages of Sivaganga district in Pulikanmai village also a Local Community Organisation (LCO) is functioning and Kudi (family membership) and village assembly system are practiced. The Kudi is the family membership in the Local Community Organization. The Local Community Organisation consists of Kudi (family membership) village assembly and village executive committee. Families having land in the irrigated area of the tank are called farming Kudi. A family without land is called a general Kudi. In the past SC families were not taken into the Kudi system. In recent years SC families with land in the irrigated area are admitted into the Kudi system.

A Kudi membership register is maintained in the village. Every year in the month of July the Kudi register is updated. The Kudi members form the village assembly. The village assembly has about 10 meetings in a year. The village assembly has an executive committee. Before 1977 traditional leaders from prominent families formed the executive committee. From 1977 a new system of selection of members for a period of one year by rotation was introduced. The village assembly selects five members in the month of September to the executive committee.

The executive committee is responsible for the day-to-day management of affairs related to the village and irrigation tanks. They collect contributions, ensure participation in various activities related to tank maintenance, proper distribution of water and management of water scarcity.

**Diagram 8.1 :** Pattern of Irrigation

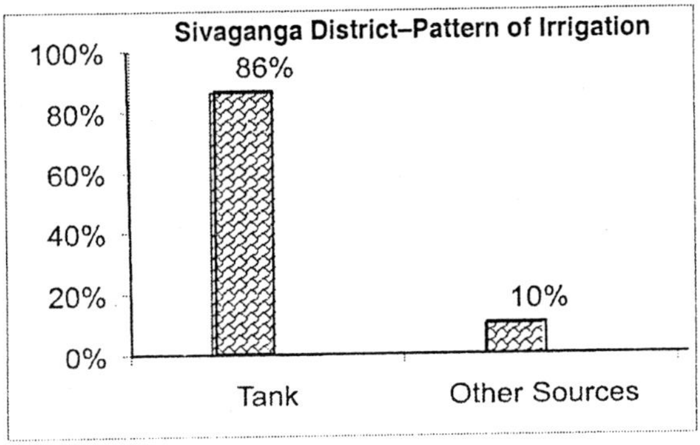

## Participatory Management of Irrigation Tank

The Kudi system facilitates participation of people in the management of irrigation tanks effectively. It is a self-governing system without any external inducement or incentive. The system has been sustained for hundreds of years. The system ensures the livelihood security of the people of the village. Particularly during the years of reduced rainfall, but for the system, people could not save their crops and have food security. The chance of crop failure is very much reduced. During water scarcity people are able to share water, change the cropping pattern and save the crop. Here the major activities of the Kudi system are discussed.

**Diagram 8.2 :** Types of Irrigation Tanks

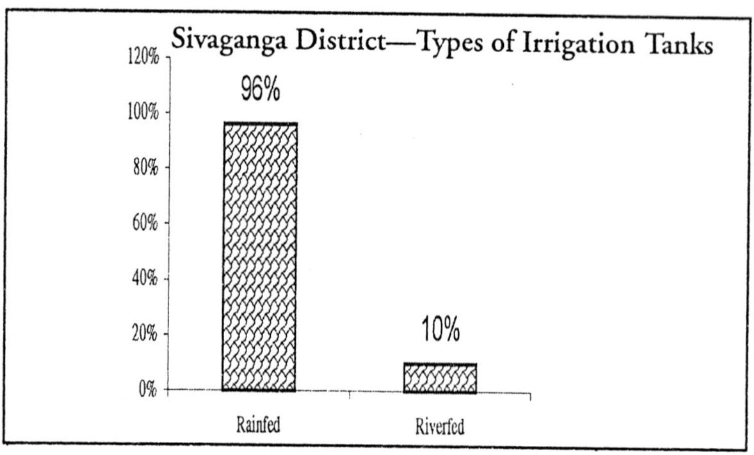


### (a) Kudimaramathu (Community Maintenance)

As in many other villages in Sivaganga and Ramnad Districts, the people in Pulikanmai village regularly undertake Kudimaramathu. Vivasaya Kudis in the village take the responsibility of doing Kudimaramathu. Kudimaramathu in the village has the following functions:

(1) Clearance of supply channels,
(2) Desilting the sluice areas,
(3) Clearance of field channels.

Before the onset of the monsoon, a special meeting to discuss Kudimaramathu work is conducted. The meeting decides the date and the time of the work.

Normally the clearing of the supply channels is done in the month of August. For the annual clearance work every Kudi has to contribute labour. Every Vivasaya Kudi has to send one person with required implements for the work and both men and women are accepted. In case a Kudi is not in a position to send a person it can send a labourer as an alternative. On the same day the silt around the sluices of the supply channels are removed and it is ensured that the sluice is in good condition. In one single day the clearance work is done. Clearance of the field channels is also done on a fixed day before opening the water for irrigation.

### (b) Disaster Management and Participation in Emergency Repair of Tank

During the rainy season and floods, the entire Pulikanmai village carefully watches the flood situation. The common irrigators, farmers and executive committee members take great care to prevent tank breaches. In case of overflow of water, specific measures are taken as precautionary measures. In the year 1995, there was a breach in the tank. All the families were asked to come to work with empty jute bags. Each family was required to bring at least two such jute bags. Around two hundred men, women and children were engaged to repair the breach in the tank. Around three hundred jute bags filled with sand were used in the operation. Within four hours the entire operation was over. The cost of the operation could be around one thousand rupees. It is impossible for any State agency or Panchayat to meet such an emergency situation mustering people's participation.

## (c) Distribution of Water

Water is a scarce commodity in Pulikanmai village. Water in the tank has to be economically used and coordination among the users is required to save water. In case there is no control over the use of water, the chances for crop failure are high. In view of this the farmers of Pulikanmai have the practice of taking collective decisions regarding water distribution in their village assembly. The village assembly decides the date for opening the sluices. It appoints two common irrigators. The appointment of common irrigators helps the people to overcome difficulties in water distribution to the fields. Two common irrigators can take care of the irrigation to all the fields served by the tank. Individual farmers are relieved of their responsibility of irrigating their farms. As the common irrigators are experienced people, they can use the water more efficiently and economically than other individuals. Conflicts over use of water, particularly in times of water scarcity, are also reduced by the presence of common irrigators. Common irrigators are well aware of the rules, regulations and customs relating to the distribution of water. As the common irrigators have to collect their wages from the farmers, they ensure proper water distribution. The performance of the common irrigators is also monitored by the farmers and deficiencies, if any, or mismanagement is reported promptly to the executive committee.

## (d) Scarcity Management

Water scarcity is a frequent problem in Pulikanmai. Water scarcity may result in damage to the standing crops. To mange water scarcity, the people of Pulikanmai have developed from experience a method of collective management. Food security and equity are the two basic principles governing the strategy for managing water scarcity. Water is considered a common property of the village and every Kudi is assured minimum water supply to ensure minimum harvest. To manage acute water scarcity, special village assembly meetings are held. Depending on the availability of water, the area to be cultivated is determined. If the tanks is filled only to half of its capacity, the assembly allows the farmers to cultivate only 50 per cent of the landholding of the Kudis. Kudis having less than 50 cents are permitted to irrigate their entire land area. If the water scarcity is acute, another system, viz., Kudi Eevu or share of the Kudi is followed. In this system the concept of equity in water use is followed. Each Kudi is permitted to irrigate only a small piece of land (about 50 cents) to avoid crop failure and fulfilment of minimum food requirement of the community. The size of the land holding of the individual is not taken into consideration. In this system small and marginal farmers are benefited. But indirectly, the large farmers are also benefited. Because unregulated use of water without any planning at a time of water scarcity may result in crop failure and economic loss. The theoretical problem of Hardin's tragedy of commons is skilfully avoided by the participatory approach of the Kudi system of Pulikanmai.

### (e) Community Fishing

As per the rules the right to harvest fish in the Panchayat irrigation works must be given on lease to generate income for the Panchayat. In Pulikanmai village, the LCO has taken the responsibility of using the irrigation tank in the village to regulate fishing in the tank for the benefit of the entire community. Individual fishing or unauthorized fishing in the tank is strictly prohibited.

The executive committee members negotiate with the Panchayat and, as per the Government rule, they pay the minimum fee prescribed and avoid public auction. On a date fixed by the village assembly, the tank is opened for community fishing. A member from each Kudi is permitted to enter the tank for fish harvesting. Within three hours the harvest can be completed. The next day onwards people are allowed to fish in the tank without any restriction. For nearly a week, people can get fish for personal use. The system regulates the behaviour of the community for the entire year and permits them to harvest the benefit collectively by the year end. Every family in the village gets fish for nearly for a week in a year.

## (f) Conservation of Trees

The people of Pulikanmai are aware of the importance of conservation of the watershed for the health of the irrigation tanks and the ecology of the village. Conservation of trees and the regulation of grazing are the twin policies followed by the LCO. The trees in the tank and in the common lands are under the control of various Government Departments, the Panchayat and the Panchayat Union. But, in Pulikanmai, regulations have been imposed by the LCO to conserve the trees in the village. Two guards have been appointed in the village to prevent any unauthorized cutting of trees. The entire village has taken the responsibility of protecting the trees. Any unauthorized cutting attracts penalty by the village assembly. Abundant thorny bushes are available in the common lands of the village for fuel for the community.

## (g) Regulation of Grazing

The LCO has imposed restrictions on grazing to conserve the top soil, to avoid silting of the tank and for the conservation of plants. Such restrictions are discussed in the village assembly and decisions are taken. At present, the following two types of restrictions are imposed on grazing:

(1) Rearing or grazing of goat is strictly prohibited within the village land area,
(2) Grazing permits are issued by the LCO for cattle other than goats.

Goat rearing is a profitable income generating activity in rural areas. Pulikanmai village has abundant vegetation which is favourable for goat rearing. But the villagers have collectively imposed a ban on goat rearing, as goat rearing is considered a great threat to top soil, vegetation and conservation of trees.

Grazing by other animals is also restricted and stall feeding is practiced in the village. During summer, when getting fodder is difficult, grazing permits are issued to cattle other than goats. From this practice the village generates resource for the local community fund. In the year 1996-97, the village could collect around Rs. 5000 from issuing permits for grazing. People strictly follow the rules relating to goats. If a goat is purchased for the purpose of meat, it cannot be kept by a household for more than a week and violation of this rule will attract a penalty.

## (h) Activities for Collective Good

Wade argues, "In the South Indian context at least, villagers are likely to follow joint rules and arrangements only to achieve intensely felt needs that could not be met by individual response. These are likely to be concerned primarily with the defence of production (avoidance of crop or animal loss), secondarily with the enhancement of income, and finally (and a long stretch from the first two) with education, nutrition, health and civic consciousness".[14] The LCO, which is primarily concerned with the management of natural resources, is also able to generate participation in the form of labour contribution, monetary contribution and adherence to prescribed rules for the development of the village in the following areas.

The villagers of Pulikanmai have decided to ban liquor (sale or use) within the boundaries of the village. The mismanagement of the Government- run Noon Meal Centre was collectively challenged by the people. The LCO tried to correct the corrupt organizers of the Noon Meal Centre by persuasion. The food materials and eggs of the Centre were not properly distributed to local children by the Noon Meal Organizer who had political patronage. The LCO repeatedly made several representations to the higher officials and finally got the Noon Meal Organizer transferred from the village. Around Rs.700 was spent from the village common fund for arranging this transfer. The village did not have a ration shop. The villagers had to walk two kilometres to collect their ration goods from a nearby village. The village assembly decided to take efforts to bring a ration shop to the village and authorized the executive committee to take necessary steps and to spend money for the purpose from the village common fund. The executive committee worked hard for nearly two years to get sanction for the ration shop. A sum of Rs.1600 was spent from the village common fund for this common purpose.

A local library and reading room was a felt need in the village. In a meeting of the village assembly it was decided to get a Government Sponsored local library in the village. For starting a local library, as per Government Rule, a minimum number of people have to take membership by paying the prescribed fee and the local community has to contribute a share of the expenditure on establishing a library. The village assembly spent Rs.22,000 on the supply of chairs, tables, books and payment of membership fee. Within fifteen days all the requirements for starting a rural library were fulfilled by the LCO. In the same way, the village has constructed a building in the local secondary school by its efforts. The Kudis were asked to provide a person each to work in the construction project. The expenses on materials for the construction were met from the village common fund. Around Rs.15,000 worth of materials and Rs.10,000 worth of a labour were contributed towards the construction of the school building.

The village has the practice of collectively contributing to funeral ceremonies. In case of a death, every Kudi has to pay Rs.10 and around Rs. 1200 is immediately mobilized. The collection is given to the bereaved family. At least one member from each Kudi has to attend the funeral ceremony. It is an arrangement of social security and display of communal solidarity. Such social action brings people together and personal conflicts and differences of opinion among families are reduced by such repeated processes of community action. It builds a base for harmony and cooperation among families for development work.

The LCO of Pulikanmai also operates a micro credit system. The major portion of the community fund is offered for credit to its members. In the year 1996-97, Rs.25,000 was distributed from the community fund among 50 Kudis at an interest rate of 36 per cent.[13] As the interest rate was high, only people with real need took the loan and repayment was very prompt.[15] The income generated from the credit system was recycled again and again into the credit system. Normally the commercial money-lender charges not less than 60 per cent. The common fund in the village gives a helping hand to the families in the village during emergencies and saves them from the clutches of money-lenders.

## Assurance Provided by the LCO

As discussed earlier, 'assurance' is the key factor in facilitating collective action for the management of natural resources. Institutions are required to coordinate and predict the behaviour of individuals in the context of collective action.[16] If an institution can give sufficient assurance and if the participants are profited by their contribution, the scope for participation is high. In Pulikanmai village the farmers want to avoid crop failure due to crop water loss. Use of water without any restriction or coordination may result in crop loss. Such crop loss will ruin their economy. This is a key factor which influences the people of Pulikanmai to enter into an institutional framework. As per the law, the tank has to be managed and water has to be distributed by the Panchayats. But, in practice, not only in Pulikanmai, but also all over Tamil Nadu, the Panchayats do not undertake any such work.

In Pulikanmai, under threat of economic loss, people have developed a regulation of behaviour and an institutional arrangement to coordinate behaviour. Their organization gives them assurance of efficient management of water. For managing scarcity of water and avoiding risk of crop failure, they depend on their organization. The organization, its rules and its conventions, are developed locally by the beneficiaries or stakeholders over a period of time. The organization is fully autonomous. People are sure that their organization is not controlled by any outside agency. The organization ensures that non-contributors are not permitted to enjoy common benefits created out of the contribution of the rule abiding participations and no one can enjoy a free ride. The organisation is controlled by the stakeholders and all major decisions are taken by the stakeholders. The supply of water as per the rules to the fields of the participants is ensured by the organization. Appointment of common irrigators reduces the expenses of individual farmers. It also prevents conflicts among farmers in water sharing. The Kudi system links contribution to resource sharing. Without contributing to the maintenance of the irrigation tank, one can not get water from the tank. This assurance by the institution ensures a positive behaviour among the participants conducive to cooperation for collective good.

Another important assurance given by the institution is that of equal distribution of water among all Kudis in case of scarcity. The interest of marginal farmers is also protected by this scheme. Every Kudi is assured of a minimum harvest of paddy even in a year of water scarcity. In the absence of such regulation, the entire crop in the tank area may fail in years of water scarcity.

The processes of decision-making and implementation are very simple, transparent and quick enough to meet the requirements of the people. As there is no separate official machinery for this work, the cost of transactions is minimum and the scope for corruption is limited. As sanction for expenditure is given by the village assembly and the accounts of the organisation are discussed in the village assembly the scope for any misappropriation of funds is also nearly eliminated. The account books are well maintained. As the executive committee has only one year's tenure and membership is rotated, there is no scope for dominance by any individual in organisational matters.[17]

The system has been operating efficiently for several decades. The present structure of the organisation is a modernised form of the older organisation. In the new structure, traditional leaders have been replaced by an executive committee selected for one year. There is no electoral politics in the organisation and there is no intervention by any Government Authority. Because of these reasons the organisation is stable. This stability gives assurance to the individuals on the predictable behaviour of the organisation.

The most important strength of the local organisation is the capacity to conserve and sustain natural resources for several generations. Because of the proper maintenance of the irrigation tank and other water bodies the people of the village are assured of getting a minimum harvest. The assurance given by the LCO facilitates and sustains the participation of the people of Pulikanmai in the management of natural resources.

## Conclusion

The tradition of participatory management of irrigation tanks is still found to exist in varying degrees in the villages of Sivaganga district. Participation emerges in certain situations wherein people are challenged by certain critical problems like drought, water scarcity, crop failure and floods. These factors force people to take collective steps to solve their common problems. In such situations local stakeholders' institutions are very much required. The local institution must assure the stakeholders of its capacity to protect their interests. Particularly institutions evolved by the stakeholders based on their needs are able to provide the required assurance to the people. Restriction of membership, equity, transparency, autonomy and cost effectiveness are the key determinants of the sustainability of local institutions for tank management. It is very much encouraging to see that still thousands of locally evolved little organisations are able to protect and manage small irrigation tanks ignored by the State system. The activities of such little organisations reveal the potential for participatory institutions.

### NOTES

1. Tamil Nadu Panchayats Act 1994, Section 133, Government of Tamil Nadu.
2. V. Ragupathy, *Participatory Management of Natural Resources*, New Delhi: Concept Publishers, 2003.
3. E. Ostrom, *Governing the Commons: Evolution of Institutions for Collective Action*, New York: Cambridge University Press, 1990.

4. M.Oslon, *Logic of Collective Action: Public Goods and Theory of Groups,* Cambridge: Harvard University Press, 1971, pp.1-2.
5. R.Wade, *Village Republic: Economic Conditions for Collective Action in South India,* Chennai: Orient Longman, 1987, pp.30-31.
6. G. Hardin, *The Tragedy of Commons,* Science, 162, 1968
7. V. Ragupathy, *Local Community Organisations in Sivaganga District,* Gandhigram, 1999.
8. Moose David, *Local Institutions Ecology and History in South Indian Tank Irrigation,* Wales: Centre for Development Studies, University of Wales, 1996.
9. *District Revenue Profile,* Collectors Office, Sivaganga 2004.
10. *Ibid*
11. *Ibid*
12. Group Discussion with Members of the Village Assembly LCO, Pulikanmai, May, 1998 all the details given on LCO.
13. LCO Records Pulikanmai, 1997 all the details regarding LCO of Pulikanmai are gathered from LCO Records of Pulikanmai.
14. R.Wade, *Op.cit,* p.221.
15. Pulikanmai LCO Accounts Book 1996-97, Pulikanmai: LCO, 1997.
16. Hardin, *Op.cit.*
17. Discussion with LCO Members, Pulikanmai, 1999.

# Index